The People Behind SCHOOL SHOOTINGS AND PUBLIC MASSACRES

John A. Torres

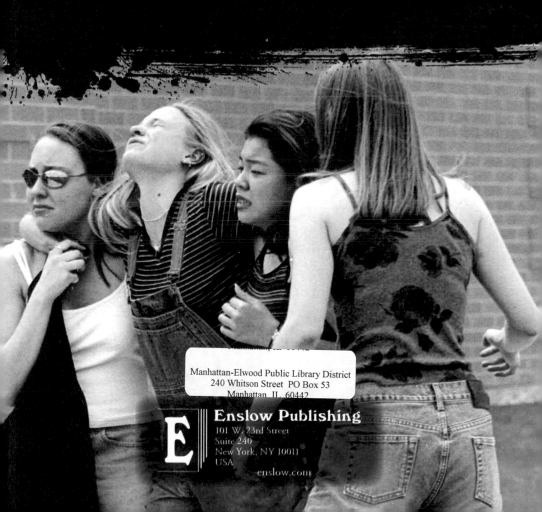

E Enslow Publishing
101 W. 23rd Street
Suite 240
New York, NY 10011
USA
enslow.com

Published in 2017 by Enslow Publishing, LLC.
101 W. 23rd Street, Suite 240, New York, NY 10011

Library of Congress Cataloging-in-Publication Data
Names: Torres, John Albert, author.
Title: The people behind school shootings and public massacres / John A. Torres.
Description: New York : Enslow Publishing, 2017. | Series: The psychology of mass murderers | Includes bibliographical references and index.
Identifiers: LCCN 2016005594 | ISBN 9780766076150 (library bound)
Subjects: LCSH: Murderers—Psychology—Juvenile literature.
Classification: LCC HV6515 .T67 2016 | DDC 364.152/34092273—dc23
LC record available at http://lccn.loc.gov/2016005594

Printed in the United States of America

To Our Readers: We have done our best to make sure all website addresses in this book were active and appropriate when we went to press. However, the author and the publisher have no control over and assume no liability for the material available on those websites or on any websites they may link to. Any comments or suggestions can be sent by e-mail to customerservice@enslow.com.

Photo Credits: Cover, pp. 1, 31, 61, 64, 109, 112 © AP Images; throughout book, chrupka/Shutterstock.com (scratched black background); Merkushev Vasiliy/Shutterstock.com (red background), Tiberiu Stan/Shutterstock.com (brain waves); p. 7 Mario Tama/Getty Images; p. 9 A. and I. Kruk/Shutterstock.com; p. 14 w:User:Jtmichcock/Wikimedia Commons/AndrewKehoe.jpg/public domain; p.16 Source unknown/Wikimedia Commons/kehoe sign.jpg/public domain; p. 19 Maxger/Shutterstock.com; pp. 23, 24 Shel Hershom/The LIFE Images Collection/Getty Images; p. 28 ROBERT LABERGE/AFP/Getty Images; pp. 35, 46 MARK LEFFINGWELL/AFP/Getty Images; pp. 38, 41 Jefferson Country Sheriff's Department via Getty Images; p. 49 HECTOR MATA/AFP/Getty Images; p. 52 Buyenlarge/Moviepix/Getty Images; p. 57 New York Daily News Archive/Getty Images; p. 66 GAylon Wampler/The LIFE Images Collection/Getty Images; p. 69 Arapahoe Country Sheriff's Office/Handout/Getty Images; p. 73 Todd Sumlin/Charlotte Observer/TNS via Getty Images; p. 78 Zubovich/Shutterstock.com; p. 81 Carol Guzy/The Washington Post/Getty Images; p. 82 Chip Somodevilla/Getty Images; p. 86 DON EMMERT/AFP/Getty Images; p. 89 Helen H. Richardson/The Denver Post/Getty Images; p. 93 JOHN MACDOUGALL/AFP/Getty Images; p. 96 Sean Gallup/Stinger/Getty Images; p. 101 Scott Olson/Getty Images; p. 104 ODD ANDERSON/AFP/Getty Images; p. 106 Jeff J Mitchell/Getty Images.

Contents

Traits of a Mass Murderer [1]

1. *Seeks revenge.* In 30 percent of mass killings, family members are the main victims. The next most likely target is the workplace, to take revenge on a boss or coworkers. Some mass murderers blame society and open fire in public places, or they target police.

2. *Has access to high-powered weapons.* Daniel Nagin, a criminologist at Carnegie Mellon University, says, "It's technologically impossible to kill a lot of people very quickly without access to assault weapons."

3. *Blames other people for his or her problems.*

4. *Often has a mental illness, particularly paranoid schizophrenia.*

5. *Is a loner, with few friends or social connections.*

6. *Carefully plans the attacks, taking days to months to get ready.*

7. *Has suicidal tendencies.*

8. *Has made violent threats, to the target or others indirectly, prior to the attack.*

9. *Is often reacting to a stressor just prior to the rampage, such as the loss of a job or a relationship.*

10. *The actions are not often a surprise to those who know him or her.*

INTRODUCTION

It is not easy to understand murder. It is even more difficult when the killing seems random and the victims innocent. We use words like horrific, gruesome, barbaric, and insidious to describe some of the crimes perpetrated by our fellow human beings on one another.

We expect a level of comfort and safety in our lives. We might expect danger while wandering lost in the rough part of town, but never do we expect to have to dodge bullets while we are out shopping at the mall or enjoying a cheeseburger at our favorite fast-food restaurant. Parents never expect that their children will be shot and killed after they are dropped off in the morning and sent on their way with a full backpack and bagged lunch. That kind of stuff is not supposed to happen. But when it does, the victims' families are left bewildered by the kind of person who can commit such violent acts.

For centuries, experts have tried to figure out why it happens. We call the killers monsters. In Mary Shelley's novel, *Frankenstein*,

Dr. Frankenstein's creation, the creature built out of different human body parts who goes on a killing spree, is called a monster. But at first the nameless being is timid and gentle and—like all of mankind—wants to feel accepted and part of society. He is shunned because of his grotesque appearance and the violence begins. Frankenstein's monster is not simply a metaphor for a victim of bullying and alienation but also of mental illness. Remember the story? Dr. Frankenstein's intention was to supply his creation with a superior brain, one of a learned man. Instead, the creation ends up with the brain of a deranged or mentally ill man.

Being bullied, shunned, alienated, and despised was not a good combination for a mentally ill person in Shelly's classic story. That remains true today. When Seung-hui Cho massacred 32 of his classmates at Virginia Polytechnic Institute and State University—known as Virginia Tech—in 2007, he left behind scary, rambling notes and videos that revealed his violent fantasies and tortured mind.

"You have vandalized my heart, raped my soul, and tortured my conscience," he says on a video. "You thought it was one more pathetic life you were extinguishing. Thanks to you, I die like Jesus Christ to inspire generations of weak and defenseless people."[2]

Clearly, Cho was suffering from some deep-seated feelings of rejection and alienation. But it was also revealed that he had previously been accused of stalking women and had checked into a mental health facility. Like Frankenstein's monster, Cho's actions were a combination of his environment and his biology.

So, what else do we know about these people that go out—many times with a plan—to shoot and kill unarmed people? One thing many have in common is their gender. "The vast majority of the perpetrators are male; by our count, females instigated only

A candlelight vigil marked the one-year anniversary of the shootings at Virginia Tech, the deadliest school shooting in US history since the 1800s.

four of the 101 school shootings that have occurred worldwide since 1974."[3]

We also know that the shootings often start as secret fantasies. But hasn't just about everyone secretly dreamed of taking revenge on those they feel have wronged them? Yes. And as a matter of fact, psychologists say that it is absolutely normal, and even healthy, to do so, as all fantasies can help spark creativity and intelligent thinking. The darker fantasies can accomplish even more.

Almost everyone has imagined vengeful scenarios, even murderous ones, after particularly frustrating experiences, according to research by psychologist David Buss of the University of Texas at Austin. Such fantasies can defuse tension and, thus, might be considered a type of psychological hygiene. As Austrian psychoanalyst Theodor Reik put it, "A thought of murder a day keeps the psychiatrist away."[4]

Now we know the typical school shooter or mass murderer is a male who has harbored secret fantasies of revenge and murder. But that doesn't really narrow it down all that much. What happens next does, however. While most people keep their darker fantasies to themselves, those who wind up acting out their anger and misplaced vengeance have difficulty keeping their feelings secret. Whether it's confiding in their closest friends, writing in journals, or posting their feelings on social media, they start to share. Many criminologists view this as a call for help. They don't really want to go out and kill; they would rather be stopped, noticed, and helped. Recognizing the signs of such deadly thoughts, as opposed to harmless daydreaming, can enable parents, teachers, social workers, and other trusted adults to head off trouble before it begins.[5]

While these dark fantasies can be cleansing and helpful to many, they can be too much to handle for someone with mental illness. A mentally ill person may grow obsessed with the fantasy and start to rationalize the need to act on it. Some of the warning signs include the person starting to become more withdrawn, preferring to be alone, and shunning social situations. That's because they begin to prefer their new, dark fantasy world to the real world and their real relationships. This behavior can be more dangerous than it seems, especially if the person has been bullied or teased, has low self-esteem, and feels as though the future holds nothing good for him.

Another warning sign is that sometimes these future killers become fascinated with others who have acted on their murderous

People who act out their anger tend to share their dark thoughts. They may write the feelings in a journal or tell their close friends.

fantasies or even some of the most brutal and murderous dictators—like Hitler or Stalin. They interpret their idols as having resorted to violence in order to be respected. The narcissistic thinkers never consider their intended victims. It's only always about themselves. That narcissism sometimes manifests itself in a savior complex. The killers think they have reached some sort of understanding or equality with God or a god.

The Columbine High School killers—Dylan Klebold and Eric Harris—proclaimed themselves as gods who should be feared. This allowed them to feel they were not subjected to the laws of society and behavior that most follow. And Cho's video message proclaimed his murderous act akin to the sacrifice made by Jesus Christ. The warning signs are often there and go unnoticed. But psychologists still have a long way to go in understanding what causes people to go over the edge and commit these atrocities.

The next chapters will take a closer look at some of these mass killings at schools or public places. The intent is not to glorify these horrific deeds, but to determine if there were any obvious causes that might have been identified before the killers took action. And let's always remember the numerous innocent victims who were in the wrong place at the wrong time.

Chapter 1

Older Cases of

SCHOOL SHOOTINGS

While it's true that the Columbine High School shooting changed just about everything to do with school security and how gun control and bullying are viewed, it wasn't the first deadly attack on a school filled with students. Far from it. Unfortunately, history is pockmarked with incidents of murderous violence in the world's schools. Since the first public school was opened in the 1600s in this country—though it was a British colony then—schools have too often been the site of unspeakable violence.

We have been battling the issue of school violence since the 1700s. Incidents include students killing students, lovers' quarrels gone wrong, teachers shooting teachers, random strangers shooting children, bombs on school property, and accidental shootings.[1]

The first school was opened in 1635 and for more than a hundred years there were no cases of murderous school violence. Back then only boys could attend schools and weapons were not allowed on school grounds.

The first incident of school violence was a case of a small school house in Pennsylvania simply being in the way of a skirmish during the Pontiac Rebellion—when Native Americans of the Lenape tribe were at war with early colonists. One afternoon in July 1764, fighters from the Lenape tribe ran into the school and began to slaughter its inhabitants. The schoolmaster, Enoch Brown, and 10 children were killed. Others were injured but survived the onslaught. Native American women and children were killed in retribution. This first school massacre was caused by bad politics and warfare, not the aggressions of a sociopath.[2]

The Indian attackers were branded as cowards by even their own tribe. Three Indians who created the massacre angered the tribes. A memorial was dedicated to Enoch Brown and the children with a stone pillar and a gravestone placed near the schoolhouse's location.[3] The attack was thought to be only a legend for many years until a mass grave containing the bodies of the students and Enoch Brown was discovered.

The fact that the attack was political in nature and merely an act of terrorism during war keeps it from making the list of attacks in this book. Many of the early accounts of killings involve revenge killings of teachers for being too harsh, and one case involved a teacher who strangled a student to death because he killed the teacher's sparrow.

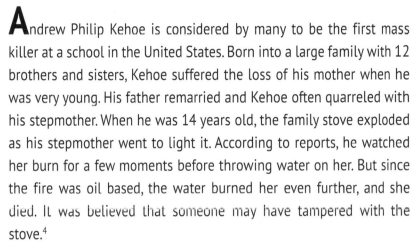

Born: February 1, 1872

**Occupation: Farmer and treasurer
of school board**

Died: May 18, 1927, suicide

Andrew Philip Kehoe is considered by many to be the first mass killer at a school in the United States. Born into a large family with 12 brothers and sisters, Kehoe suffered the loss of his mother when he was very young. His father remarried and Kehoe often quarreled with his stepmother. When he was 14 years old, the family stove exploded as his stepmother went to light it. According to reports, he watched her burn for a few moments before throwing water on her. But since the fire was oil based, the water burned her even further, and she died. It was believed that someone may have tampered with the stove.[4]

Kehoe went to school for electrical engineering, where he met his future wife. Somewhere between college and starting a farm in Bath Township, Michigan, Kehoe suffered a fall and a head injury. It is unclear how much, if any, effect that had on his personality, which had grown angry.

Kehoe wasn't very good at farming and continually borrowed money from his wife's aunt to keep the farm afloat. He blamed everyone but himself for his bad fortune. To his credit, he did try to act peacefully to fix his bad luck. Believing the high taxes he

13

Financial difficulties, a violent temperament, and anger at the cost of school taxes led Andrew Kehoe to perform the deadliest school massacre in US history.

was paying were to blame for his misfortune, Kehoe decided to get involved and be a part of the solution.

Kehoe became obsessed with school taxes, especially when there was talk about building a new school. He became so riled that he ran for a position on the school board and became the board treasurer. The problem was that he started working so much on trying to stop the new school that he neglected his farm. It went to waste.[5]

Despite all of Kehoe's work, dedication, and complaining, the new school project was approved. This absolutely infuriated Kehoe, who was prone to anger and violence. He once shot a neighbor's dog for barking too much. He also chased a priest off his land and then forbade his wife from attending services. He also used to get into regular arguments—even over small things—with other members of the school board. He rarely agreed with them or voted their way.[6]

By the morning of May 18, 1927, things had reached a desperate point for Kehoe and his family. He had fallen so behind in paying back his wife's aunt that she had informed him that she had no choice but to repossess the property.

He snapped. He killed his wife with a shovel and then went around the farm destroying every fruit tree that he had. His dead wife's aunt was entitled to the land, but he wasn't going to give her the farm. He killed the animals, then went to his work shed and fashioned a plaque that he hung on the fence outside his farm.

Next, Kehoe placed dynamite under his home and throughout the buildings on his property. He then sat on his porch and watched the children walk past his property to the nearby school. Nearly an hour after the school day commenced, Kehoe's farm blew up. The farm was destroyed. But then, things really got devilish. Knowing that the town's leaders would gather at the nearby school

CRIMINALS ARE MADE, NOT BORN.

After killing his wife, Kehoe made this sign and placed it on his farm's property.

after hearing the explosions, Kehoe loaded his car with explosives and drove to the school. He proceeded to blow himself up along with the school. His bombs killed forty-three people at the school and injured nearly sixty others.

It would be a while before everyone discovered what was written on the sign he made. It read: "Criminals are made, not born."

Danger signs:

Cruelty to animals, anger issues

Pattern of attack:

Mainly bombs

Number of victims:

Forty-five including his wife and himself

Born: September 24, 1883

Occupation: Teacher

Diagnosis: Suffered a mental breakdown

Died: 1932, from tuberculosis while in an asylum

German national Heinz Schmidt moved to Bremen, Germany, with his mother in 1912. He did not know it at the time but she moved there to try to have her son admitted to a mental hospital. He had lost a successful teaching position a few years earlier when he suffered a mental breakdown. He spent time in a sanatorium but was released and declared cured. He wasn't, and his mother knew it. Others did too.

After moving to Bremen, Schmidt began buying a large number of weapons and thousands of rounds of ammunition. The gun sellers became so concerned they actually contacted the police about him. But very little was done.

Before his last and deadly breakdown, Schmidt had begun harboring an intense hatred for the Jesuit order. Jesuits are an order of Catholic priests who take a vow of poverty and whose main work is in education. For example, Fordham University in New York is a Jesuit-run university. For some strange reason he blamed the Jesuits for his father—a Protestant pastor—getting very sick. He started writing letters bashing the Jesuits and calling for their disbandment. Knowing this, it is little surprise his target was a Jesuit school, St. Mary's, in Bremen.

In 1913, Schmidt shot students at St. Mary's school in Bremen, Germany.

The final straw in this troubled man's mind was the death of his chronically ill father on Thursday, June 19, 1913. The next day, he went to the school armed with between six and ten pistols; murder on his mind. Shortly before 11 a.m., teacher Maria Pohl was working to get her students lined up in two orderly lines to go outside for recess. That's when Schmidt ran up the stairs and opened fire at anyone who was in his way.[7] Panic followed as two girls were shot dead immediately. Another tried to climb a railing to escape but fell and broke her neck. The little girls, who were only five and six years old, pleaded with the killer to stop shooting. "Please don't shoot us," they called.[8]

Upon hearing the shots, some teachers barricaded their doors and ordered the children to jump out the second floor windows into the courtyard below. A janitor jumped on Schmidt's back to try to stop the onslaught but received a bullet through the jaw. A teacher who also tried stopping Schmidt was shot in the chest and killed. Schmidt shot and wounded several boys that tried escaping through the courtyard.

By this time, many parents had heard the shooting and were running toward the school. They grabbed Schmidt and nearly beat him to death. The police came and arrested him but had trouble protecting him through the night as a lynch mob had formed outside the police station. The mob demanded that Schmidt be turned over, but the police drove them away. Eventually, Schmidt was deemed insane and spent the rest of his years in an insane asylum. He died of tuberculosis in 1932. The Bremen school massacre is considered the first school attack in German history.

Danger signs:

Had recently lost job and was distraught

Pattern of attack:

Packed up to ten guns and went to the school intent on killing

Number of victims:

Five

Born: June 24, 1941

Occupation: Bill collector/student

Diagnosis: Brain tumor may have
affected his actions

Died: Killed by police on August 1,
1966

It would be more than a century after Kehoe's rampage before another mass murder that claimed more than ten lives occurred at a school. This time it was the infamous Charles Whitman, whose story has been the subject of numerous media portrayals since August 1, 1966. It was on that day that Whitman climbed to the top of a tower at a crowded university and decided to pick off students one-by-one with a high-powered sniper rifle. When all was said and done, the twenty-four-year-old former Marine had claimed sixteen lives.

Born in Florida, Whitman was the oldest of three boys. His father was a good provider and made sure the family had food, a roof over their heads, and nice clothes. But in return, he was a strict disciplinarian who physically and emotionally abused his wife and children. It did not seem to have an effect on Charles at the time, however, as he proved himself to be a bright student with a keen intellect at a very young age.

Moreover, Whitman was actually the ideal child. He took on a job delivering newspapers. He joined the boy scouts and was reportedly the youngest ever to achieve the rank of Eagle Scout.

Taught by his father how to shoot and maintain guns, he became an avid marksman and expert hunter. There didn't seem to be anything he couldn't do well.

He graduated near the top of his high school class but enlisted in the US Marine Corps right after graduation in order to get away from his overbearing and abusive father. He did well initially in the armed services, earning recognition as a sniper; he even qualified for a program that allowed him to go to college.

But when his grades did not meet the necessary requirements, his superiors demoted him and took away his schooling. Whitman was devastated. He started drinking and gambling and got into trouble for his gambling more than once. Upon his honorable discharge, he enrolled in the University of Texas at Austin to pursue an architectural degree.

But his world changed in 1966. Whitman's mother and brothers left his father for good, unable to endure any further abuse. During that time, Whitman was under great stress and started experiencing terrible headaches. He was also abusing amphetamines. It was shortly after midnight on August 1 that Whitman's stress, headaches, and drug abuse culminated in murder. He drove to his mother's nearby home and stabbed her in the heart. Before he killed anyone, Whitman composed a note.

"I don't really understand myself these days," he wrote. "I am supposed to be an average reasonable and intelligent young man. However, lately (I can't recall when it started) I have been a victim of many unusual and irrational thoughts."[9]

He then went home and killed his wife in her sleep, leaving a note beside her body saying he loved her more than anything and that he did not know why he was doing these things. Whitman knew

Charles J. Whitman was an ideal child, but after his grades dropped in college, he began gambling and abusing alcohol and drugs. He also suffered from very painful headaches.

Charles Whitman opened fire on strangers from this tower at the University of Texas at Austin, seen here through a bullet-pocked store window across the street.

something was seriously wrong and said so in his suicide note. In the letter, he asked that an autopsy be done on his body to see if something had changed in his brain. He felt that it had.[10]

He spent the next few hours preparing for his onslaught. He bought several guns, a scope, extra ammunition, and a dolly. Then he proceeded to drive to his school—the University of Texas at Austin. He took the elevator to the twenty-seventh floor—the closest he could get to the top of the clock tower. From there he began shooting anyone in his field of vision. The police tried shooting him from a plane but could not. Finally, a few brave officers entered the tower, went up twenty-seven flights and shot and killed Whitman.

An autopsy was performed, and a commission later determined that a brain tumor likely influenced Whitman's actions, causing the headaches and the violence.

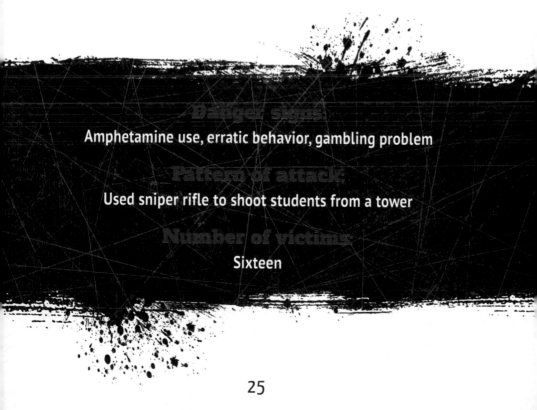

Danger signs:

Amphetamine use, erratic behavior, gambling problem

Pattern of attack:

Used sniper rifle to shoot students from a tower

Number of victims:

Sixteen

Born: Gamil Rodrigue Liass Gharbi on October 26, 1964

Occupation: Part-time hospital worker

Diagnosis: Personality disorder

Died: December 6, 1989, suicide

Like several of the other killers profiled in this book, Marc Lépine of Canada hated his father. It wasn't that Lépine's father demanded too much, but rather because he abandoned his family. First, the Algerian moved his young family around a lot. They lived in Costa Rica and Puerto Rico for a while before going back to Montreal, Canada. Eventually, Lépine's father left his wife, son, and daughter—but only after passing along his utter contempt and hatred of women to his son. The Lépine children had to live with relatives during the week as his mother had to work to support him and his sister. He would see her only on the weekends.

Lépine's father had physically abused Lépine's mother and by the time he was only 16 years old, the reclusive, withdrawn boy legally changed his last name to his mother's: Lépine. He said he wanted nothing to do with having his father's name. There were warning signs in school, and maybe today they would have been recognized and addressed.

For kids in need of help, a thoughtful response to the problem is essential. School psychologists and social workers need to help disillusioned youths find a place for themselves in society, something many of them feel they lack. Earning that respect might take the form of finding a job or an activity that they enjoy and in which they excel. On a broader scale, schools can offer seminars that advise students on ways to discover their talents and interests and how to use them to earn admiration.

With no such programs or mechanisms in place, Lépine continued to become withdrawn. He also started to get angry. He began thinking like his father, harboring feelings of contempt for women. This led to him resenting his younger sister, who forever taunted and teased him about his severe acne and social life. Things got so bad that he used to fantasize about killing her and once even created a mock grave for her.[11]

By the time Lépine reached young adulthood, he was dealing with several problems. First, he seemingly could not find a girlfriend. Secondly, he wanted to attend École Polytechnique in Montreal but was not admitted. Lastly, he was struggling with work. He was fired from the job his mother had helped him get because of a poor attitude, and he then had to move back in with his mother. He could not find a job he wanted. Lépine resented women taking on what he felt were jobs that should traditionally go to men. By this point, he was blaming women and feminism for everything that had gone wrong in his life.

On December 6, 1989, he walked into a second-floor classroom at the École Polytechnique in Montreal brandishing a gun. He separated the men from the women and started killing the women. He shot and killed fourteen women before turning the gun on himself.

Police psychiatrists did extensive work on this case after his suicide. They examined his letters and writings, and interviewed

Anne St-Arneault's name forms one of the fourteen plaques unveiled on the tenth anniversary of the Montreal Polytechnic massacre where fourteen women, including St-Arneault, were killed by Marc Lépine.

family and his few friends. They found that Lépine likely suffered from extreme personality disorder, which, more often than not, manifests itself in a homicidal/suicidal fantasy or reality.[12]

His mother told authorities that perhaps his hatred of feminists was a way of acting on his resentment toward her for her getting a job, pursuing a career, and neglecting him. We will never know.

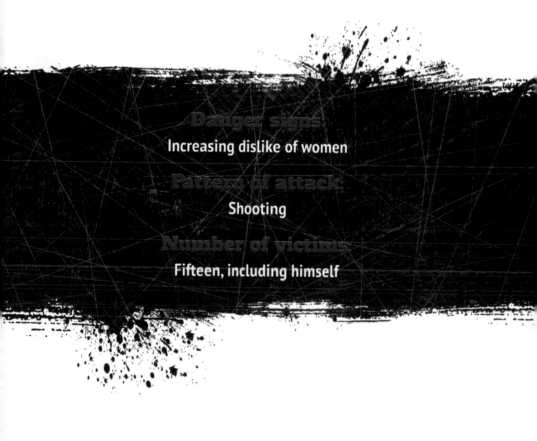

Danger signs:
Increasing dislike of women

Pattern of attack:
Shooting

Number of victims:
Fifteen, including himself

Thomas Hamilton

Born: **May 10, 1952**

Occupation: **Youth club organizer and shop owner**

Died: **March 13, 1996, suicide**

The case of Thomas Hamilton and the school shooting massacre he perpetrated in Scotland is significantly different from the other cases discussed in this book. Hamilton shares the lack of a real father with some of the other killers, though he did not realize it while he was growing up.

His strange childhood began in Glasgow, Scotland. His mother had already divorced his father by the time he was born. Society back in the 1950s did not look kindly upon and was not accepting of single mothers. So, with that in mind, Hamilton was raised by his mother's parents. They actually adopted him by the time he was two years old, and he believed they were his parents. He also grew up believing that his true mother was actually his sister.[13] He did not learn the truth until he was twenty-two years old.

Not much else is known about his childhood. He was reportedly an above-average student who enjoyed shooting rifles and handguns as well as scouting and camping. However, it was not long before many started discovering that his involvement in scouting was really to feed his attraction to young boys.

Thomas Hamilton burst into the Dunblane Primary School in Scotland on March 13, 1996. He opened fire with four handguns, killing sixteen children and their teacher.

When he was only in his early twenties and serving as an assistant scoutmaster, there were numerous complaints that Hamilton was engaged in illicit behavior with some of the young boys. He liked taking photographs of them in their underwear or bathing suits without their parents' permission. There were also complaints of Hamilton forcing some of the younger scouts to sleep in his van with him while they were on camping trips.

He was banned from the scouts in 1974. This was crushing to him, but he did not let it impact his attraction. Instead, Hamilton started up his own clubs over the years. In fact, at one point he had sixteen very successful boys clubs. But his true nature too often came out, and eventually membership numbers declined.

The boys whom he ordered to run around in their underwear and bathing suits called him "Mr. Creepy" and laughed at him behind his back. Even the adults secretly called him names, referring to him as "Spock" because he seemed so different. Others said his face and voice made their flesh crawl.[14]

He was described as a loner who was often abrasive and intolerant of others. He had few friends outside the circles of young boys. And while four different police agencies in Scotland investigated claims of improper behavior with boys, Hamilton was never arrested or charged with a crime. In fact, even as the rumors grew over the years, many parents came to his defense. Hamilton denied the rumors saying they were started by the scouting organizations because of his success.

The rumors, however, hurt his business and his behavior became more erratic. Had he ever really acted on his impulses? Or did he simply like to take pictures of semi-clothed boys? On March 13, 1996, everything came to a head. Only a few days earlier, Hamilton fired off letters to politicians, newspapers, and basically anyone who might listen, complaining bitterly about the rumors and how they had ruined his life. They took on the tone of suicide letters. Hamilton drove to Dunblane Primary School where he proceeded to shoot everyone in a classroom. He shot twenty-eight of twenty-nine in one classroom and actually killed seventeen: one teacher and sixteen young children.

He then turned the gun on himself.

Danger signs:

Attraction to young boys; growing resentment

Pattern of attack:

Shooting

Number of victims:

Eighteen, including himself

Chapter 2

COLUMBINE

They say America lost its innocence and feeling of being a special nation when President John F. Kennedy was assassinated in 1963. Nothing would ever be the same again. Other countries looked at us differently, and we looked at ourselves differently. Something was lost forever. The same can probably be said for April 20, 1999.

People often talk about where they were the day Kennedy was killed. The same can be said about the Columbine High School massacre. It certainly was not the first school shooting in America, but it was the first one that the public was able to follow on live television as the drama unfolded. It was also the first that involved cell phones, meaning more information emerged from victims and survivors in real time. As a nation, we were glued to our televisions, mesmerized and horrified that something like this could actually happen.

After Eric Harris and Dylan Klebold started their shooting rampage, bomb squads and SWAT teams secured students.

School security was never the same. People started taking bullying seriously, and school safety and gun control became regular topics on the nightly news. For months and years, psychologists and criminologists have worked to figure out why this attack that changed America occurred.

The mainstream media reported that Eric Harris and Dylan Klebold acted out in such a murderous fashion because they had been bullied so much. The answers lie much deeper and are more complex than simple bullying. After all, not every person who has been bullied becomes a murderer. In fact, hardly anyone who is bullied becomes a murderer. Harris and Klebold were bullied, to an extent. That's a fact. But they were doing some bullying of their own as well.

"Harassment was not a one-way street," said noted psychologist Peter Langman, who extensively studied school shootings — especially Columbine. "Eric engaged in his own harassment of other students. In fact, Eric, Dylan, and other boys threatened and intimidated another student to the point that he was in tears and afraid to attend school. Thus, Eric was not only a victim of harassment, but a perpetrator of harassment, too. He had a bad temper and there were many students who were alienated by his belligerent behavior."[1]

When documents and reports were made public a decade after the attacks, a more complex picture emerged of the two killers. That, as well as the scope and magnitude of the Columbine massacre and what it has meant since (even for future school shooters), is why this incident warrants its own chapter.

The killings ignited a national debate over bullying, but when records were released to the public years later, it was revealed that Harris and Klebold bragged in their diaries about picking on freshmen and homosexuals.[2] So what did the documents, letters, journals, and videotapes reveal? The first thing they revealed was how little we actually knew about the killers and their reasons when this initially happened.

Ten years after Harris and Klebold made Columbine a synonym for rage, several books were published that included new information released for the first time. Some of these books analyzed the tragedy through police records, interviews, diaries, e-mails, appointment books, videotapes, and other sources. What was learned? Well, that just about everything we had been told regarding the shootings was wrong.[3]

Instead, a portrait emerged of two cold-blooded, misguided teens who were not targeting jocks, Christians, African-Americans, or bullies at all. They had hoped to kill everyone in the school, including their friends.

This goes beyond bullying. When the pair—clearly led by Eric Harris—started shooting, they did not target those who in their minds had wronged them, but they fired indiscriminately, killing anyone in their path. And this was really only because numerous bombs they had planted around the school failed to detonate.

Harris wasn't looking to target any particular people or specific groups at all. He was interested in killing as many people as he could. That was it. Harris wanted to blow up the school. He also had bombs set up in the parking lot to try and kill parents and rescue personnel. He wanted to be remembered for killing. He wrote, "I want to leave a lasting impression on the world."[4]

Far from the low self-esteem of a perpetual doormat for bullies, Harris often portrayed himself as an elitist, even writing "I am God," in German in several of his friends' yearbooks. He had become fascinated with Adolph Hitler and often spoke of raping young girls and physically hurting them, as well as eliminating people who were intellectually disabled from the face of the earth because he deemed them inferior.

In many ways, the two boys behaved—at least around those closest to them—as most normal hormonally charged teenage boys would. But, of course, that was far from the truth.

Dylan Klebold fires a sawed-off shotgun at a makeshift shooting range in March 1999. This image is from a video released by the Jefferson County Sheriff's Department. Approximately six weeks after this video was made, Klebold and Eric Harris killed thirteen people at Columbine High School.

The truth is the killers were far from normal teens. According to psychologists who studied their behavior leading up to and including the shootings, Harris was a psychopath, and Klebold battled depression. Still, they weren't representative of the extreme social outcasts and loners depicted in the early days of media coverage.

According to records released by the Jefferson County Sheriff's office, Harris and Klebold had their own circle of friends. Klebold even took a date to the prom, riding with a dozen friends in a limo, only a few days before the shooting.[5] Neither Harris nor Klebold ever mentioned bullying in their diaries.

Psychologists have called Harris a cold-blooded psychopath who had everyone fooled. He achieved good grades in school. He loved to read, and his essays were above average. Many described him as the type of kid who knew exactly what to say around adults in order to hide his true feelings.

Harris, according to psychologist Peter Langman, who wrote a book about Harris and Klebold, was a ticking time bomb who had already committed many crimes including theft, credit card fraud, and vandalism. He also said Harris fantasized about blowing up the entire city of Denver and crashing a plane into New York City. This was several years before the 9/11 terrorists did just that.

Klebold, on the other hand, had been diagnosed as suffering from depression and suicidal thoughts. He was lovelorn and lonely and wanted to be accepted. He found that acceptance in Harris, who often drew swastikas in his journal while Klebold drew hearts.

It is interesting to note that psychologists have studied more than the killers, their behavior leading up to the gruesome crime, and the victims. They have also studied the public's perception and why, all these years later, the general public believes Harris and Klebold were trench coat-wearing killers who targeted those who bullied them and acted out only after years of oppression. Those initial notions have all been debunked, yet perceptions have not changed.

Psychologists who study memory have said that the general public tends to remember first impressions. With regards to Columbine, what the public first saw and heard in the news tended to stick with them.

Professor Elizabeth Loftus at the University of California-Irvine, who specializes in memory, said, "Myths continue to be validated when people start talking with others about an event. Once memories are embedded, people resist changing their minds."[6]

The Day of the Shooting

Wanting their actions to rival the Oklahoma City bombings from a few years earlier, Dylan Klebold and Eric Harris woke for school on April 20, 1999, with murder in their hearts. This was not a spur of the moment action. The two had planned this for more than a year and even saved most of their money from after-school jobs in order to buy weapons, ammunition, and the components to build bombs. They started filming videos and writing journals, which contained clues that this may have been part of a larger attempt to act out their fantasies of escaping to Mexico and one day destroying Denver and New York City.

The morning of April 20, they planted bombs away from the school, near the fire department. The idea was that they wanted to distract rescue personnel, giving them more time to inflict their carnage at the school. They left a bomb-filled duffel bag in the

Columbine shooters Eric Harris, left, and Dylan Klebold appear in this video capture of a surveillance tape in the cafeteria at Columbine High School during their shooting spree.

cafeteria, then went outside to the school parking lot and waited. When it did not blow up, they decided to enter the building and start shooting.

Born: April 9, 1981

Occupation: Student

Diagnosis: Treated for anger and depression; possibly suffered from narcissistic personality disorder

Died: April 20, 1999, suicide

Eric Harris, believed to be the mastermind of the Columbine school shooting massacre, was born in Wichita, Kansas, but it was never really home. Two years later, the family moved to Ohio. It was the first of many moves, but such is the life of a military family. His father was a decorated air force pilot who excelled at testing strategic missiles and space defense systems. He was known as a strong leader, and by all accounts Eric looked up to him greatly and often expressed a desire to follow in his footsteps.[7]

Eric's father often spent all of his free time with Eric and his older brother. In fact, when the family moved from Ohio to Michigan, his father became a scoutmaster and played basketball with his sons whenever he could. Aside from the constant moving, Eric Harris seemed to have a happy childhood.

When the air force base in Michigan was shut down, the family moved to upstate New York, where his father was assigned to a base in Plattsburgh. It was the sixth different base that Major Wayne Harris had been assigned to. Harris attended middle school and reportedly had friends of every race, which makes it even more curious why his pre-Columbine videos and writings contained hatred toward minorities.

Eventually, as rumors swirled that the Plattsburgh base too was going to shut down, Harris's father decided to retire and move the family to a pristine area with crisp, clean air—Littleton, Colorado. Eric's older brother, Kevin, thrived at Columbine High School. He played football, enjoyed popularity, and then went on to study at the University of Colorado.

The first real outward sign that Eric may have been mentally unstable was a few days after a freshman homecoming dance. He had taken a girl who later told him she did not want to be his girlfriend. He reacted by faking his own suicide and staging it for her to see.

By sophomore year he had shown signs of resentment toward the popular football players at the school and mainly kept to himself and made friends with many of the unpopular kids. He started spending more time playing online shooter games. He also found a job at a local pizzeria and started making his own money. He often complained of loneliness and bemoaned the fact that he didn't have a girlfriend.

It was at the pizza shop that he met a fellow high school student who had the same shyness and loneliness issues he had. His name was Dylan Klebold. The two became inseparable. They began engaging in minor criminal mischief together, like stealing signs or lighting firecrackers. But soon these pranks began to take on a more serious nature and even a military-style feel. They called the pranks missions and would target neighbors who they felt were rude or dismissive.

They burned down bushes and glued doorknobs. Once Harris was caught, he seemed to become unhinged. He began a revenge plot to destroy his school. He started drawing diagrams of the school in his personal journals, and his Internet writings and journal were filled with hate.

He went to a psychologist for depression, anger, and suicidal thoughts. Records and sources indicated that Harris was taking the prescription drug Luvox, which is most commonly used to treat obsessive-compulsive disorder and depression. Mixing Luvox with alcohol could cause extreme agitation, and Harris was apparently fond of drinking Jack Daniel's whiskey.[8]

His mood darkened. He and Klebold would talk about minorities and how they wanted them dead. They became more and more racist and obsessed with guns and the military. A few days before the Columbine attack, Harris tried to enlist in the US Marines but was rejected because he was taking medication. No one is really sure how much of a role that played in the massacre, but some believe that he stopped taking the medication that day and fell into an even darker place.

Two nights later, while many at the school were enjoying the senior prom, Harris stayed home, dateless. He showed up at the school later on, after the dance, when casino-style games were being played. He acted inappropriately, causing a scene. Because of his behavior, teachers asked him to leave. He could no longer use his charm and wit to mask the evil intent of his heart or his mental instability.

Most who have studied the case agree that Harris was a ruthless, cold-blooded psychopath, and like so many other psychopaths, he felt superior to others.[9] He felt he was entitled, and when he did not get the things he wanted—a girlfriend, acceptance, and entrance into the marines—he viewed them as personal slights and insults. He needed to get even, to make things right. Other theories, based on some of Harris's own journal entries, suggest his lack of success with girls and the fact that he was still a virgin, may have played a bigger part in his actions than previously thought.

Eric's journal reveals a lot of sexual frustration and anger at the girls who rejected him. He wrote a lot about self-hatred and lack of confidence too. "If people would give me more compliments all of this [the attack] might still be avoidable.... You know what, maybe I just need to [have sex]."[10]

That fateful morning, when the bombs did not detonate, a furious Harris led Klebold into the school where they shot and killed

Students from Columbine High School watch as the last of their classmates are evacuated from the school building.

twelve students and a teacher. They went room to room, taunting and yelling and shooting indiscriminately. The duo even went to the cafeteria to shoot the bombs they had made in another effort to get them to detonate. They wounded more than twenty students before heading to the school's library where they wounded more. By this time, the school was in pandemonium and police had surrounded the building. Students were running to safety.

The pair shot at police through the windows before deciding it was over. There would be no Denver destruction or New York's demise at their hands. Instead, they yelled "one, two, three" and shot themselves.

Danger signs

Hate-filled journals and writings

Pattern of attack

Shot fellow students

Number of victims

Fifteen including himself and his partner

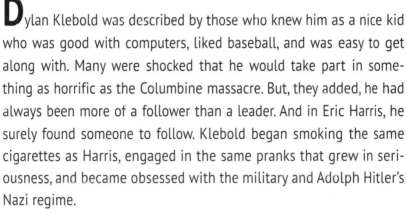

Born: September 11, 1981

Occupation: Student

Diagnosis: Depression

Died: April 20, 1999, suicide

Dylan Klebold was described by those who knew him as a nice kid who was good with computers, liked baseball, and was easy to get along with. Many were shocked that he would take part in something as horrific as the Columbine massacre. But, they added, he had always been more of a follower than a leader. And in Eric Harris, he surely found someone to follow. Klebold began smoking the same cigarettes as Harris, engaged in the same pranks that grew in seriousness, and became obsessed with the military and Adolph Hitler's Nazi regime.

Friends said that during weekly Friday nights at the bowling alley, Klebold would yell "Heil Hitler!" every time he rolled a strike. This turned off a lot of classmates, especially since his own mother was part Jewish. Other friends never really knew if he truly admired the Nazi doctrine or was simply trying to outrage friends with some tasteless humor.

Klebold's parents—Tom and Susan—named Dylan after one of their favorite poets, Dylan Thomas. The young family settled into a $400,000 home in an upscale suburb near the high school. Eventually the Klebolds quit their jobs and started a property rental company. They were doing quite well. There were no signs during his childhood that would lead anyone to believe that Dylan would one day be a mass murderer. He joined the Boy Scouts and played Little League baseball. Family friend Vicki DeHoff said Klebold's parents showed their two children a lot of love. "They didn't neglect them. They were caring, concerned, funny, loving, kind, involved," she said.[11] Years later, DeHoff's daughter would survive the Columbine nightmare when she hid in a closet as the two teens walked through the hallways shooting.

Before any of the criminal mischief started, Dylan was the model student and seemingly perfect son. In fact, his parents often commented to neighbors how he wished his older son was more reliable and responsible like Dylan. He was known as one of the brightest kids in school, often finishing assignments weeks in advance. He was also friendly and kind, something that Harris wasn't. Klebold would often sneak cookies to his classmates.

"Dylan wasn't a bad guy," said former classmate Jennifer Harmon, one of the regular recipients of Klebold's cookie treats. "I never thought he would do something like [the rampage]. But they said Eric's name on TV and I automatically knew Dylan was going to be there. Eric had a persuasion. I think Eric would always tell Dylan that people never liked him, and he was his only true friend."[12]

The duo even wrote about the same things during a creative writing class. They would spin yarns about zombies, violence, carnage, killings, and weapons. But most of their classmates enjoyed it, thinking they were trying to be funny. No one really took them seriously. Some have speculated that right up to the moment of planting the bombs in the school's cafeteria, Dylan may have believed the entire plan was still just a fantasy.

If someone has been planning what would surely be a suicide mission for April 20, then why would they bother spending hours meticulously drafting a fantasy baseball team just a few weeks earlier? But that is exactly what happened. Unlike Harris, who showed no real mainstream interests, Klebold was obsessed with baseball—as a fan, not a participant. He even made roster moves on his fantasy team right up until just a few days before the massacre. While Harris has been described as psychopathic, what can be said of the follower Klebold, the boy who would seemingly do anything to impress Harris? It's difficult to characterize killing people as foolish.

Littleton residents stand near a carpet of flowers, mourning those who died at Columbine High School.

But how else can you explain why someone would go against their own nature to kill and harm others, crush his parents—whom he loved—and throw away his own life just to impress a friend? [13]

Klebold's mental illness has been called mild and placed in the psychotic category. Langman said that Klebold had a "'schizotypal' personality disorder, a condition bordering on—but not yet quite at—the level of psychosis, although sharing some features, such as disordered thinking and language processes, feelings of persecution, and a distorted self-image."[14] Whatever the diagnosis, it is hard to understand how Klebold went along with the plot. Just one week before the killings, Klebold and his father spent one week at the University of Arizona touring the school. Klebold liked it so much that his father even put down a deposit on the tuition and dorm room for his son. That all changed on April 20, 1999.

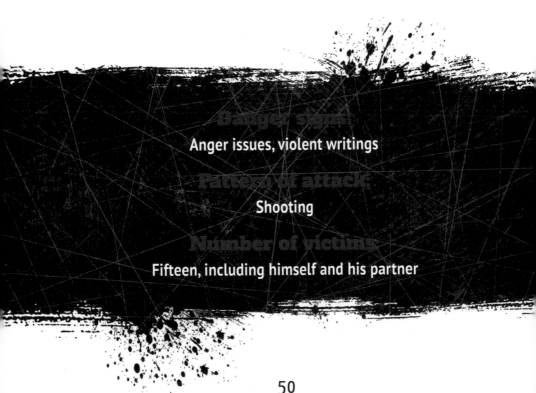

Danger signs:
Anger issues, violent writings

Pattern of attack:
Shooting

Number of victims:
Fifteen, including himself and his partner

Chapter 3

Going

POSTAL

We've all heard the term and maybe used it ourselves. "Going postal" has become part of our lexicon, a phrase used to describe someone snapping and losing it, becoming uncontrollably angry after enduring a bad situation for as long as they were able. The 1995 film *Clueless* is credited with popularizing the phrase and helping it go mainstream, though several newspapers had already used the phrase.

The reason for the phrase was a rash of shootings and killings at US Post Offices by disgruntled workers between 1986 and 1993. And even though the post office remains one of the safer places to work, the shootings were so high-profile that the idea of a postal worker losing his cool became something the public latched on to. The term has taken on a comedic or jokelike quality over the years, though it is steeped in horrific murders and scenes of carnage. It is even used in sports to describe an athlete who just made a good, aggressive play or whom the other team cannot control.

The 1995 film *Clueless* helped popularize the phrase "going postal."

The term, the phenomenon, and the crimes can be traced back to Patrick Sherrill, who was the first letter carrier to lose his cool and commit murder. Now, just about any workplace shooting or public massacre is described as someone going postal. But what about the science? Many of us have had to work at jobs we hated or experienced unbelievable stretches of bad luck that make us want to "lose it," or at least make us feel as if we cannot take one more day of it. The result is normally not mass murder.

There exist numerous theories about what might drive a person to commit such horrific acts. But these people all seem to have one thing in common. They all lack the internal controls needed to regulate their anger and allow them to deal with conflicts in a rational manner.[1]

Is it genetics or learned behavior? What is it that causes some to be able to cope and others to "lose it?" Some believe the behavior is in direct correlation to bad parenting. Maybe children just are not being disciplined enough. Maybe they are growing up with a false sense of entitlement. The thought is that there is too much emphasis on rewarding good behavior and not enough emphasis on punishment. Punishing bad deeds can be a great motivator to learn self-control and do the right thing.

The question has to be asked over and over: Why is it that so many people these days appear to have failed to develop such controls? Even normal people seem capable of going berserk when over-stressed. Maybe it has something to do with how we—as a society—are instilling discipline in our children.[2]

Of course that is only one angle or theory in a thoroughly complex issue. Another involves whether or not it is good or healthy to "release steam" or allow the anger to manifest itself in order to keep it from boiling over into something worse. For years that theory, known as catharsis, was thought to be a helpful and appropriate way to deal with anger issues.

Sigmund Freud, who believed in catharsis, said that all repressed fury could build up and fester before exploding into hysteria or violent aggression. He believed the solution could be found in releasing the anger and negative feelings in a controlled manner.[3] But this has proven to be false. Many studies have revealed that feelings of anger and hostility grow when individuals act on their anger—perhaps by taking it out on a punching bag or screaming into a pillow. The idea, psychologists say, is to express anger in small doses, but rely mainly on communication to get to the bottom of the issue and try to come to an understanding that will not end in violence.

What neither theory considers is that the person perpetrating the violence, the person unable to contain himself, may be suffering from an untreated mental illness. As you will see in this chapter, several killers were suffering from one mental disease or another, and one in particular just could not cope with how his life had turned out.

> **Born: November 13, 1941**
>
> **Occupation: Postal worker**
>
> **Diagnosis: Anger management issues; possible factitious post-traumatic stress disorder**
>
> **Died: August 20, 1986, suicide**

Patrick Sherrill was known as Crazy Pat long before he walked into the post office in Oklahoma where he worked with the intention of killing everyone in sight. Born in Oklahoma in 1941, Sherrill was always a little different. He was quiet and preferred his own company to anyone else's. He was not very popular in school, but he also was not considered an outcast. His high school friends remembered a stocky, shy loner who worked hard at sports, earned three varsity letters, and even started on the high school football team's defensive line.

One high school friend described Sherrill as having the expression of "a lonely, abandoned child" in his eyes, yet a bravely smiling countenance. "Nobody could have been as shocked as I was at what happened," said Don Roberts, now of Houston, who was the quarterback on Pat Sherrill's old team at Harding High School.[4]

In 1963, when President John F. Kennedy was assassinated, Sherrill enlisted in the US Marines. He became an expert in weaponry and a skilled marksman while serving as a sniper for the military while the country was embroiled in the Vietnam War. However, he was never deployed to Vietnam, serving his entire military career in the states. But, after leaving the military, Sherrill led everyone to believe that he had indeed seen combat in Vietnam. It was a way for him to feel important, but it became a dangerous game.

After his time in the marines, he joined the air force reserves and tried to become an instructor, but little things seemed to impede him. He was known to have a short fuse and a hot temper. Rumors persisted that he was a homosexual.

According to psychologists who analyzed his actions and life leading up to the massacre, Sherrill may have suffered from factitious post-traumatic stress disorder. This was a phenomenon that vets dealt with after returning from Vietnam. They were looked down upon by society and were made the scapegoats for a country in trouble. Vets who had returned from other wars were respected and honored. Vietnam was different. Sherrill started identifying with those who fought and suffered. He began to act even stranger than normal. He made obscene phone calls to women in his neighborhood. He was caught staring into strangers' windows. There was even a rumor that he was getting into trouble at work because he had exposed himself to a female colleague.

Sherrill worked as a part-time postal worker for the US Post Office. He was known to be a very good employee, hardworking, and conscientious. Speculation aside, what we know for sure is that on August 19, 1986, two supervisors called Sherrill into a back conference room and gave him a tongue-lashing. This was a common tactic at the time for USPS supervisors to get more out of already hardworking employees.

Sherrill did not appreciate it. He called his union representative and asked for a transfer. He went home shaken and angry, but only after telling a female coworker who he was fond of that she should

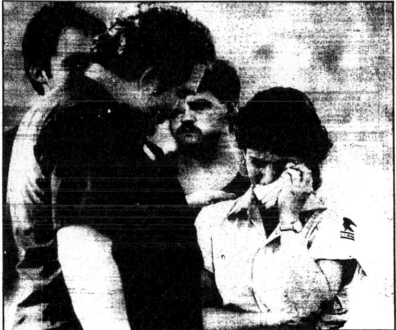

MANHATTAN + SPORTS FINAL

DAILY ◉ NEWS

35¢   **NEW YORK'S PICTURE NEWSPAPER®**   Thursday, August 21, 1986

CRAZED POSTMAN KILLS 14

SLAUGHTER

Employe of Edmond, Okla., post office is comforted after disgruntled postal worker Patrick Sherrill killed 14 co-workers and wounded six in shooting spree. Gunman then killed himself.

STORIES ON PAGES 4 AND 5; OTHER PICTURES IN CENTERFOLD

The front page of the August 21, 1986, *New York Daily News* probably stay home the following day. He stewed all evening about what had happened. He thought he was going to be fired.

The following morning, Sherrill arrived on time for his morning shift, but instead of mail in his pouch it was packed with guns. He marched straight back to his supervisor's office and shot him dead. He then went through the building, methodically shooting at his coworkers. He killed fourteen and wounded seven in less than fifteen minutes. Satisfied with what he had done, Sherrill turned the gun on himself, and it was over.

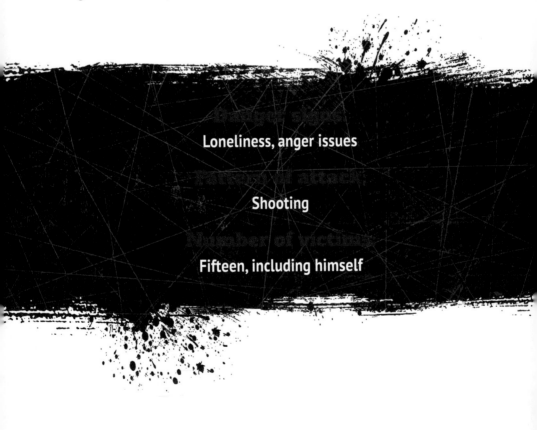

Danger signs

Loneliness, anger issues

Pattern of attack

Shooting

Number of victims

Fifteen, including himself

> **Born: January 21, 1921**
>
> **Occupation: Unemployed**
>
> **Diagnosis: Paranoid schizophrenia**
>
> **Died: October 19, 2009, of natural causes in a nursing home**

In the midst of committing mass murder, Howard Unruh took a break for a few minutes at his home and even answered the telephone. The editor of the local newspaper was calling.

"Why are you killing people?" the editor asked.

"I don't know," Unruh replied.[5]

He hung up the phone and continued his twenty-minute reign of terror, which would later become known as "the walk of death."

Not much is known about Unruh's childhood. He was born in 1921 to a Jewish father and a Christian mother. He was raised by his mother after his parents separated along with his younger brother James in East Camden, New Jersey. He graduated from Woodrow Wilson High School in 1939 with aspirations of becoming a government employee. Instead, he went into the service to fight during World War II.

Unruh was reportedly assigned to a tank during the war and was a part of the deadly and brutal Battle of the Bulge. He was known to have been brave, and he made it out safely—but maybe not soundly. It was reported shortly after the murder spree that

Unruh kept meticulous records of his time in Germany. He recorded an oddly detailed entry for every man that he killed.

When he returned from the war in 1945, he decorated his room in war and military memorabilia. He enjoyed shooting, and his mother allowed him to use the basement of their New Jersey home as a shooting range. But something was off about him. Howard came back from the war with a hollowed-out look in his eyes. Both his brother and his father noticed the difference.

Unruh's brother, James, said later that "since he came home from the service, he didn't seem to be the same. He was nervous." His father, Samuel, said his son had "built a shell around himself we could never penetrate."[6]

Unruh was admitted to a pharmacy program at Temple University but dropped out after only three months. He lived with his mother and accompanied her to religious services at the local Lutheran church every single day. He grew easily agitated with neighbors and felt that many people were talking about him behind his back. But there might have been something else at play other than just post-traumatic stress disorder—a condition not diagnosed in those days. According to a few reports written shortly after his murderous rampage, Unruh may have been experiencing anguish and guilt over being involved in a homosexual act with a stranger. He was also getting teased by neighbors regarding his sexual orientation.

By the morning of September 6, 1949, something drastic had changed. He woke up and his mother could see a darkness in his eyes. She made him breakfast and then ran for her life when he grabbed a wrench and threatened her with it. Then he left his home with a German Luger pistol and a list of people he wanted to kill. The first stop was the shoemaker's shop.

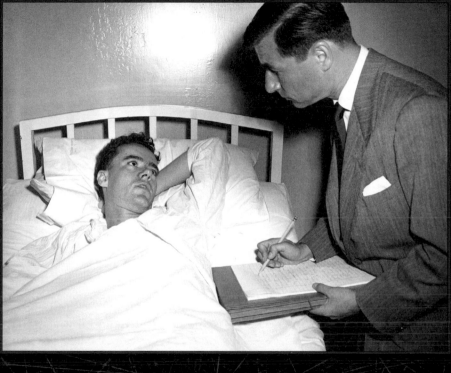

Prosecutor Mitchell B. Cohen questions Howard Unruh in a Camden, New Jersey, hospital. Unruh was sent to the hospital after he suffered a bullet wound to the hip when he barricaded himself in his apartment before being captured by the police.

"I had leveled the gun at him, neither of us said nothing, and I pulled the trigger," Unruh told a psychiatrist a month later. "He had a funny look on his face, staggered back, and fell to the floor. I realized then he was still alive, so I fired into his head."[7]

He killed thirteen people, including three children, and wounded several more. He surrendered to police when they threw tear gas into his house. He admitted everything he did and never went to trial when he was diagnosed with paranoid schizophrenia. He lived the next sixty years in a hospital for the criminally insane where he passed away.

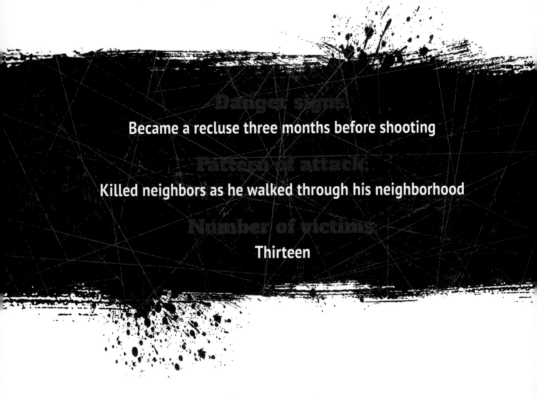

Danger signs

Became a recluse three months before shooting

Pattern of attack:

Killed neighbors as he walked through his neighborhood

Number of victims

Thirteen

Born: **October 15, 1956**

Occupation: **Unemployed merchant marine**

Diagnosis: **Racist tendencies, anger issues**

Died: **October 16, 1991, suicide**

By all accounts, George Hennard had a good childhood. His father, Georges Marcel Hennard, was a medical doctor who worked at various army bases treating soldiers and their families. This meant the family was forced to move around a lot whenever the doctor traveled to a different base. He was known to be an outgoing kid who never had trouble making friends wherever he went. He was gregarious and handsome and just about everyone his age looked up to him.

Then something happened. Can one event shape your future? It seems in this case the answer is yes. Hennard's father was a tough man, a disciplinarian, and sometimes the punishments seemed a bit harsh for the crime. One year, during junior high school, the pair got into an argument and his father beat him severely. He also took a knife and cut his son's long hair. According to friends, Hennard was never ever the same. He became quiet, introverted, and shied away from friends and girls.[8]

Hennard joined the US Navy for two years and then earned a license to become a merchant marine. But that did not last very long. While on suspension for using drugs, he got into a brawl with

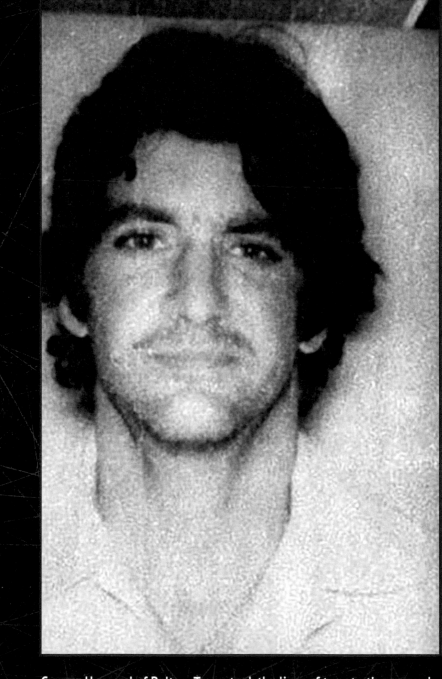

George Hennard of Belton, Texas, took the lives of twenty-three people.

a fellow shipmate who was black. Hennard called him all types of racial slurs. He was caught with drugs a second time, and his license was revoked. According to reports, his shipmates were happy to see him go. They complained of his hateful vitriol toward minorities, gays, and women.

Hennard couldn't hold down a job. He worked off the books on ships, in construction, or as a day laborer. Finally, he moved back in with his mother and started working at a cement factory. He earned enough money to move out but his anger and range continued to grow. He would often yell at the television while at a diner for lunch or while reading the newspaper.

His life, for all intents and purposes, had been a failure up until this point and he refused to accept any responsibility. It was always someone else's fault. He was angry and hot-tempered. Some described him as mean.

Sociology professor Jack Leven said some people turn to violence to fulfill the fantasy of taking back what rightfully belongs to them. "Of those who don't or can't cope in more conventional ways, a few will take their own lives," Leven said. "Unable to stand life's pressures, they seek any available means to relieve them. A very few, like George Hennard, decide to take others with them. They decide, in their own minds, to restore their status and lost pride, relieve their frustration and resentment by striking out at anybody and everybody, striking with homicidal fury at society in general."[9]

On October 6, 1991—the day after his birthday, which perhaps had reminded him how poorly his life was turning out—Hennard drove his pickup truck through the plate-glass window of a popular restaurant known as Luby's Cafeteria in Killeen, Texas. Then he pulled out two pistols and began walking around the restaurant

George Hennard's truck is removed from Luby's Cafeteria the day after he drove through the window and killed twenty-three people inside the restaurant.

shooting people. The first person Hennard shot and killed was a man who ran over to his truck to see if Hennard was alright.

There were one hundred and forty people in the restaurant and all ran for their lives. But with his truck blocking the exit, many were trapped. Hennard killed twenty-three people before taking his own life.

Danger signs:

Increasingly erratic behavior and vitriol toward minorities

Pattern of attack:

Shot people at a restaurant

Number of victims:

Twenty-four, including himself

James Holmes

Born: December 13, 1987

Occupation: Student/laborer

Diagnosis: Bipolar disorder

It's hard to imagine James Holmes without the shocking orange hair made to look like Batman's notorious villain—the Joker. But he wasn't always a murderous villain himself, a man who booby-trapped his apartment with the hopes of killing police. No, he was born in a quiet area near San Diego, California, into what seemed like a great family. His father was a scientist who earned degrees from numerous prestigious universities while his mother worked as a registered nurse.

The family moved around a bit before settling back in San Diego, where Holmes expressed interest in soccer, computers, and science. But almost immediately after moving back, when he was eleven years old, he began displaying serious signs of mental illness. He would wake with night terrors complaining that the "nail ghosts" were hammering the walls. He also saw flickering lights at the corners of his eyes.[10] He became introverted and quiet and had trouble making friends. Yet he was a brilliant student.

Resembling a character from a movie, the socially inept Holmes was able to write computer code and solve the toughest mathematical problems. He earned a degree—with honors—in

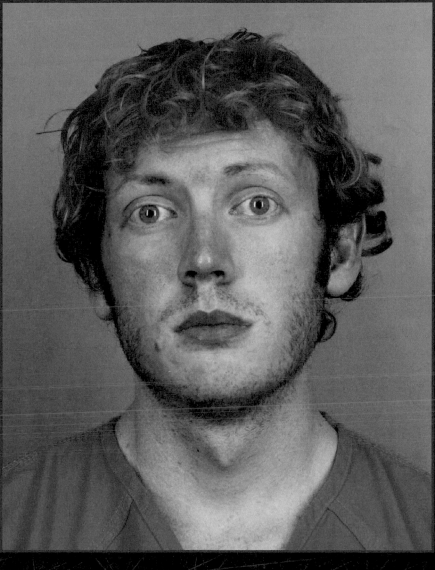

James Holmes poses for a booking photo after his shooting rampage at an opening night screening of *The Dark Knight Rises* in Aurora, Colorado.

neuroscience. He then earned a Master's degree and was enrolled in the doctorate program at the University of Colorado.

But still the problems persisted. While working at a pharmaceutical company, Holmes smirked and stared at a wall when asked if he was okay. He also had problems dating women and would often sabotage relationships by talking about death and his fantasy to kill.

Eventually the mental illness became even too great and his brilliance and grades began to falter. He was put on academic probation but then decided to resign from the program. During this time, he was seeing a few mental health professionals on campus. He was obsessed with death and killing and even sent threatening text messages to one female mental health professional who stopped treating him. The day before he became a mass murderer, Holmes sent a rambling binder filled with his thoughts about his "broken mind" to a mental health specialist.

Obsessed with Batman and the Joker, Holmes bought a ticket to the July 20, 2012, opening night showing of *The Dark Knight Rises*. Twenty minutes into the film he went to his car to don tactical gear and military clothing and to get his guns. He lobbed tear gas into the theater and began shooting.

During a mass murder, the killer often kills to strike back at their perceived tormentors, the people who have caused them pain. A mass murder will often take place after the deeply-troubled perpetrator suffers a psychotic break from reality.[11]

Unlike most mass murderers, Holmes was not suicidal. He wore protective clothing and surrendered. He admitted his guilt but entered a plea of not guilty by reason of insanity. During pretrial examinations and evaluations it was deemed that Holmes suffered from schizotypal personality disorder. He was mentally ill; there was no question about that. However, they also found him to understand the difference between right and wrong. He was found guilty and sentenced to life in prison.

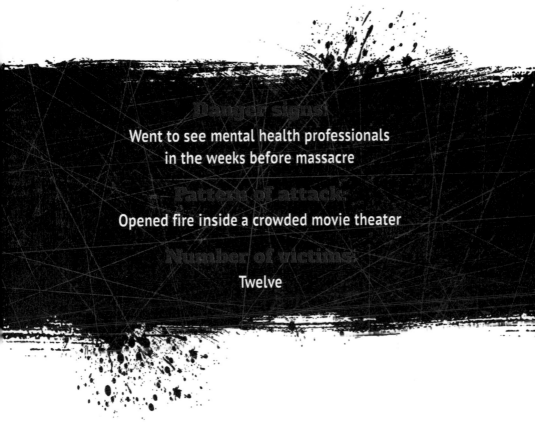

Danger signs:

Went to see mental health professionals
in the weeks before massacre

Pattern of attack:

Opened fire inside a crowded movie theater

Number of victims:

Twelve

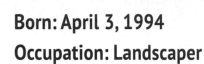

Born: April 3, 1994

Occupation: Landscaper

Diagnosis: Antisocial personality disorder

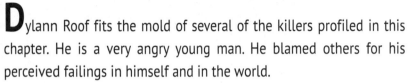

Dylann Roof fits the mold of several of the killers profiled in this chapter. He is a very angry young man. He blamed others for his perceived failings in himself and in the world.

Questions about Roof's mental health began surfacing almost immediately after he shot and killed nine African Americans inside a South Carolina church in 2015. He had to be either mentally ill or he was a racist with a gun trying to set back civil rights by 60 years.

Roof told police and friends beforehand that his intention was to start a race war between whites and blacks. But a lot of mental health experts were not buying it. Psychologists have compared that thinking to terrorism and refer back to the most important motivating factors: childhood trauma and exclusion.[12]

A look at Roof's childhood shows lots of dysfunction, but if there was any trauma then it has yet to be revealed. He was born in South Carolina in 1994. His parents—who were divorced before he was born—reconciled long enough to conceive him. They broke up again and Roof split his time between them. His father, according to reports, was verbally abusive to his new wife. They also moved

Charleston shooting suspect Dylann Roof is escorted from the Shelby Police Department.

a lot. In fact, he moved so much that he attended seven schools in nine years. It was during this stretch that the first hints of mental illness may have manifested. According to court documents, when he was about six years old he began showing signs of obsessive-compulsive behavior and was becoming a germophobe.

Both his parents struggled with their finances. His father lost his carpentry business and his mother was evicted from her apartment. In middle school, Roof started experimenting with drugs and by the time high school rolled around, the work was too difficult for him. Still, throughout his school years, Roof had many friends of different races. His mother encouraged his friendships with other races, and he was known to have some of his African American friends sleep over.

But he became withdrawn when he was forced to repeat the ninth grade, and he dropped out the following year. That's when he started looking at white supremacist websites. He began to note "black crime" and even wrote a lengthy, rambling essay on the "black crime problem." He lied to his parents about working and spent all of his time getting high, playing video games, and talking about starting a race war. He started telling friends that he was going to do something big.

On June 17, 2015, Roof walked into an African American church in Charleston and sat with a small bible study group. They were kind to him and welcomed him. He repaid them by killing nine of them.

Roof was apprehended the following day and awaits trial. The following is taken from his manifesto: "I have no choice. I am not in the position to, alone, go into the ghetto and fight. I chose Charleston because it is most [sic] historic city in my state, and at one time had the highest ratio of blacks to Whites in the country," he

74

wrote. "We have no skinheads, no real KKK, no one doing anything but talking on the Internet. Well someone has to have the bravery to take it to the real world, and I guess that has to be me."[13]

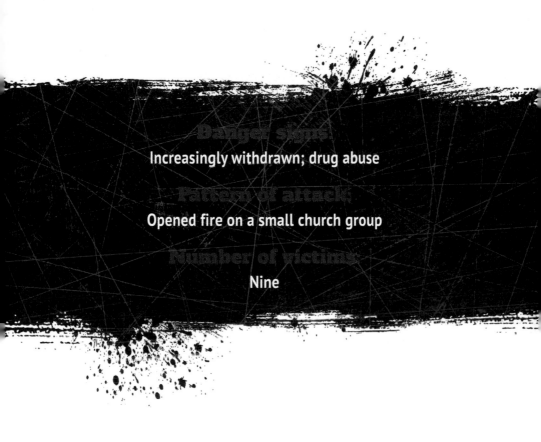

Danger signs:

Increasingly withdrawn; drug abuse

Pattern of attack:

Opened fire on a small church group

Number of victims:

Nine

Chapter 4

POST-COLUMBINE

As stated earlier, the actions of Eric Harris and Dylan Klebold changed the landscape of school safety, as well as raised the issues of recognizing mental illness and possible bullying at earlier stages, before violence occurs. There was another offshoot of the Columbine school massacre that still resounds today: copycat killings. That's right. Several school shooters over the years have even cited Harris and Klebold in their suicide notes or goodbye videos as they embark on their murderous journeys.

Why?

According to psychologist Peter Langman, learning about previous killers—like Harris and Klebold—is not likely to inspire murderous deeds alone. However, as feelings of resentment, anger, jealousy, anger, and hatred continue build, finding someone to look up to, who validates your twisted feelings, can be the final ingredient needed. Langman says, "There is often peer encouragement of some kind. Sometimes the shooters have role models for violence. They look at Eric Harris and Dylan Klebold at Columbine High School as a role model or Charles Manson or Hitler. They get into various ideologies that would support violence as appropriate. There are a lot of things coming together. But you don't have an ordinary kid who wakes up one day and becomes a mass murderer."[1]

Langman cites the little known case of North Carolina teen Alvaro Castillo, who became obsessed with Columbine. He was already diagnosed as psychotic and had attempted suicide a few times by the time he started idolizing the Columbine killers. He even tried to kill himself on the seventh anniversary of the Columbine shootings but was stopped by his father. That did not stop the psychosis. He started to believe that he had been spared for a "higher" purpose, that he should commit a Columbine-style attack. He even had his mother drive to Colorado so he could videotape the homes where Harris and Klebold once lived. There were so many warning signs that it is amazing his parents did not put an end to it or get him the help he needed. Alvarez wound up killing his own father.

Virginia Tech shooter Seung-Hui Cho was in eighth grade when Harris and Klebold killed their classmates at Columbine. He viewed them as martyrs and put them on equal footing with Jesus Christ. Cho, who went through four years at Virginia Tech without speaking to a single classmate, was obviously already troubled. But in Harris and Klebold he was able to find inspiration, brothers even. He viewed them as having been interrupted in their work and it would be up to him to complete it for them. This gave his life meaning and purpose, and it made him feel important.

Many perpetrators of school shootings fascinated by the Columbine shootings suffered from extreme isolation and had limited social interactions. They were loners who kept to themselves.

Cho is not alone. Since Columbine, there have been dozens of school shootings in the United States, and it is disturbing how many perpetrators admit to being inspired by or fascinated with the Columbine shootings. Looking back, many of them suffered through extreme isolation or had very small, poor social groups. They kept to themselves.

"So when you see that extreme isolation, this is usually with the psychotic shooters. They are having hallucinations, they hear voices talking to them, paranoid delusions, delusions of grandeur," psychologist Peter Langman told an audience at Lehigh University. "There often is a series of events shortly before the attack that pushes them over. What you see is there is some kind of an event, or they are rejected by a girl. They get in trouble at school—it may be a minor thing, but there is some kind of conflict with the school. Sometimes they get into trouble with the law, sometimes drugs or alcohol."[2]

This chapter takes a look at post-Columbine shootings, including the highly publicized Virginia Tech and Sandy Hook school shootings where the killers were indeed obsessed with Columbine.

Born: January 18, 1984

Occupation: Student

Diagnosis: Anxiety disorder, selective mutism, major depressive disorder

Died: April 16, 2007, suicide

Seung-Hui Cho was born in South Korea in 1984 and lived with his parents and two siblings in a shabby basement apartment that was way too small to accommodate a family of five. His father was a bookstore owner but made very little money.

In 1992, when Cho was only eight years old, the family set off for the United States in pursuit of the "American Dream." Like millions of immigrants before them, Cho's parents simply wanted their children to have an easier life than they had.

The family moved first to Detroit and then to the Maryland area, where they settled. Things were very difficult at first since no one in the family spoke English. His parents opened a dry cleaning business and the American Dream was on its way.

Language issues were not the only things that Cho was facing. He also started dealing with the demon of mental illness. Despite having normal interests like basketball, action movies, and video games, Cho became shy, withdrawn, and very quiet. His relationship with his father was strained. He barely spoke to his parents and avoided eye contact.[3] His teachers noticed the drastic change in

Cho's behavior and recommended counseling and art therapy. He was diagnosed with social anxiety disorder and later with selective mutism—a refusal or inability to speak when expected to do so.

His parents tried to get him more involved in extracurricular activities, but the more they pushed, the harder he resisted. Eventually, they gave up. In the eighth grade, Cho began drawing tunnels and caves, and counselors said that was a sign of depression. It got worse that April when the Columbine attacks took place. He wrote an essay saying that he wanted to commit a similar attack.

During high school, Cho's teachers set up special classes with him so he would not have to speak in public. The classes were designed for him to succeed, and he graduated with honors. Despite advice to choose a small college close to home, Cho was adamant

Seung-Hui Cho, who gunned down Virginia Tech students, is pictured in his high school yearbook picture as an eleventh grader.

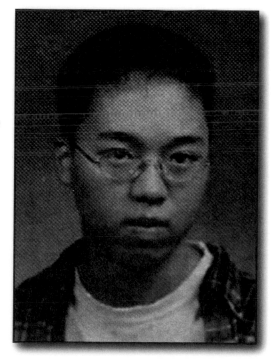

Thousands of people attend a candlelight vigil on the campus of Virginia Tech after the shooting rampage left a total of thirty-three people dead.

about attending Virginia Tech. He was very intelligent as long as he did not have to speak and was accepted into the college. But Virginia Tech officials were not informed of Cho's condition or the great lengths taken by teachers to help the young man succeed.

His first few years in college were uneventful, and he scored above average grades. But by 2005, his behavior had worsened. He started wearing sunglasses all the time, even indoors. In a poetry class, he allegedly snapped photographs of women's legs under the tables and composed violent, sex-filled poems.

His obsession with Columbine grew, and he submitted another essay about a school shooting. Stalking incidents ensued, and teachers developed codes in case something happened. They were afraid of him. At this point, Cho was in need of hospitalization. He was thought to be a danger to himself and others. But a judge did not have him committed; instead, Cho would be treated as an outpatient.

By 2007, he had amassed several guns, filmed a violent and threatening "farewell" video, and written a rambling manifesto saying that he—like the Columbine killers—was a martyr to be compared with Jesus Christ.

On April 16, 2007, a few days before the Columbine anniversary, he went to school and shot and killed thirty-two people, wounded seventeen, then turned the gun on himself.

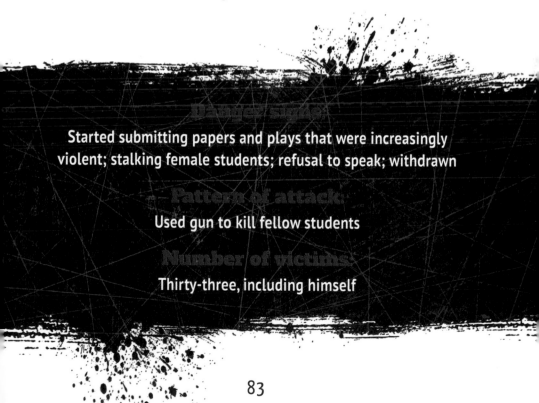

Danger signs:

Started submitting papers and plays that were increasingly violent; stalking female students; refusal to speak; withdrawn

Pattern of attack:

Used gun to kill fellow students

Number of victims:

Thirty-three, including himself

Born: April 22, 1992

Occupation: Unemployed

Diagnosis: Sensory-integration disorder; Asperger's syndrome; obsessive-compulsive disorder; possible brain damage from being malnourished.

Died: December 14, 2012, suicide

If the Columbine High School massacre shocked a nation, then the Sandy Hook school shooting devastated it. The Columbine tragedy was carried out at a high school; Sandy Hook was an elementary school.

The majority of Adam Lanza's victims were six or seven years old. They likely had no idea what was happening, let alone why. Things like this were never supposed to happen, but they absolutely never happened in Fairfield County, Connecticut, where residents had experienced only one murder during the previous ten years.

Adam Lanza lived with his mother only five miles from the school. His parents divorced when he was very young, and he was raised mainly by his mother. From the beginning, it was clear that the child had issues. Before the age of three, he was diagnosed with being significantly delayed, meaning his speech and language skills were far behind what they should have been at that age.

His first experiences in school at the age of five were marked by special education classes, him often speaking gibberish and sometimes sitting alone and banging his head on his desk, according to multiple reports. He attended Sandy Hook Elementary School for one year before his family moved and he transferred schools. He was eventually integrated into mainstream classes, but his articulation issues continued.

He was soon diagnosed with a form of autism known as Asperger's syndrome as well as obsessive-compulsive disorder (OCD). Some of his symptoms included changing his socks twenty times a day, using tissues to touch any foreign object, and blacking out the windows of his room. Lanza was also obsessed with death and military websites.

Lanza's family seemed to be in denial regarding the seriousness of his condition. Hindsight is often very clear, but this was a little boy in serious need of help and medication. At one time, his mother had told medical personnel that he was "borderline" autistic but had pretty much outgrown it.[4]

Peter Lanza, Adam's father, reflecting back on his son's childhood, said he thought his son was "a normal, weird little kid" but by the time he reached middle school "it was crystal clear something was wrong."

"The social awkwardness, the uncomfortable anxiety, unable to sleep, stress, unable to concentrate, having a hard time learning, the awkward walk, reduced eye contact," he said. "You could see the changes occurring."[5]

Psychologist Peter Langman thinks maybe the Asperger's and the OCD masked the true malady affecting Lanza—schizophrenia. "I believe that Lanza was a psychotic school shooter who suffered from undiagnosed schizophrenia. Many of his unusual traits that could be understood as belonging to an autism-spectrum diagnosis

Heavily armed state troopers leave the Sandy Hook Elementary School in Newtown, Connecticut, on the day of the shooting. Adam Lanza shot and killed twenty small children, six teachers, and his mother.

and/or obsessive-compulsive disorder could be accounted for by a diagnosis of schizophrenia."[6]

On the morning of December 14, 2012, Lanza shot his mother in the head four times and then broke into Sandy Hook Elementary, where he killed several adults and almost an entire class of first-graders before shooting himself.

Why? No one knows. But some theories are that he was jealous of the promise the healthy children had. Another theory is that he hated them because he was sexually aroused by them or even jealous because his mother once volunteered at the school, taking time away from him.

Danger signs:

Fascination with mass shootings

Pattern of attack:

Killed mother then went on shooting rampage at elementary school

Number of victims:

Twenty-eight, including his mother and himself

Born: August 8, 1988

Occupation: Student

Diagnosis: Treated for depression

Died: March 21, 2005, suicide

Jeffrey James Weise was born into a tough situation. He was the child of a very young Ojibwe couple from the Red Lake Indian Reservation in Minnesota. His parents had already separated by the time he was born. This may have been the start of a lifetime of perceived rejection. Perhaps he believed that his parents did not love him enough to stay together long enough for his birth.

While his mother went to pursue her dreams in Minneapolis, Weise was raised by his father and grandfather on the reservation. When he turned three, the young child was sent to live with his mother in Minneapolis. She married and had other children, again perhaps filling Weise's mind with feelings of being second fiddle.

Then, one tragedy after another befell the boy. His father killed himself. A short while later his mother was badly brain damaged in a serious car accident. She was sent to live in a nursing care facility.

Rather than care for and raise him, Weise's stepfather drove him to the reservation and dropped the boy off to live with his grandfather. Essentially, he was abandoned by everyone. Not that his mother and stepfather had been loving and caring while he

Red Lake Indian Reservation teenager Jeff Weise was described as a towering, young loner who always wore a dark trench coat to school. He went on a shooting spree and killed nine people including his grandfather and a woman at their home, five students, a teacher, and a security guard on the Red Lake High School campus. Then he turned the gun on himself. He suffered from deep depression and was on medication to treat it.

was living with them. Weise wrote in a blog that his mother was an alcoholic and his stepfather was abusive.

Life on the reservation was harsh. Weise lived in abject poverty in a community with high incidents of alcoholism and suicide. As a young teenager, he began acting out by skipping school, drinking, and taking drugs. His appearance changed as well as he started wearing dark eyeliner and combat boots. He was already showing outward signs of depression in 2004 when he tried to kill himself in May and then again in June of that year.

Treated with antidepressants, Weise never really got better. The drug he was taking for depression—Prozac—is believed by many to make adolescents suicidal and violent. His doctor apparently increased the dosage the week before the killings.

Weise's high school experience is a paradox. Some claimed that he was a gentle soul, a good listener, and a bright student. But at some point he became obsessed with the ideology of mass murderer and Adolf Hitler—presumably not realizing that there was no place for people who looked like Weise in Hitler's "final solution." He was expelled from school when there was a threat of a shooting there on Hitler's birthday. Weise was then homeschooled.

If Weise was quiet in school, he became an extrovert in cyberspace. It was as if he had two personalities. He may have posted messages on a neo-Nazi website expressing admiration for Hitler and calling himself "Todesengel," which is German for the "Angel of Death."[7]

He blasted women on the reservation for marrying outside their race. He also thought rap music was a bad influence on his tribe.

No one knows what caused Weise to kill. On March 21, 2005—despite reports that he was very close to his grandfather—he shot and killed his grandfather and his grandfather's girlfriend. Then he drove to Red Lake Senior High School where he opened fire. He killed a security guard and five students before taking his own life.

Danger signs

Failed suicide attempts, obsession with neo-Nazi movement

Pattern of attack

Used gun to shoot victims

Number of victims

Ten, including himself

Tim Kretschmer

Born: July 26, 1991

Occupation: Student

Diagnosis: Treated for depression

Died: March 11, 2009, suicide

The United States doesn't hold the patent on school shootings. The sad, tragic, deadly phenomenon happens everywhere.

Timothy Kretschmer dreamed of being the world's next table tennis champion. Ping-Pong was his game and he had high aspirations. He also had an inflated opinion of himself. He often smashed and threw paddles when he did not play well or win. He would berate and humiliate teammates for poor playing according to one of his coaches, Croatian table tennis champ Marko Habijanec.

When Habijanec discussed Tim's attitude with his mother, he was at disbelief to discover her siding fully with her son.[8] That seems typical of Kretschmer's entitled upbringing, according to multiple reports.

Kretschmer lived with his sister and parents in the town of Leutenbach, Germany, and by all accounts had a normal life. The family was well off due to Kretschmer's father's success as a businessman. They lived in a huge, gorgeous house and drove the best cars. The family was also well-rooted in the community, often getting involved in civic activities.

Kretschmer was treated for depression when he was sixteen— one year before he decided to steal his father's gun and shoot up a school. Some reports say that Kretschmer and his family removed him from mental health treatment prematurely—after only a few sessions. The family, however, through a spokesman, adamantly denied they ever stopped the treatments. Whatever the case, Kretschmer became withdrawn and obsessed with violent video games. He became so involved in the games that his grades began to suffer. He graduated from high school, but barely. His poor grades disqualified him from a prestigious internship he was counting on.

Like many of the other teen killers, Kretschmer appeared to be a virgin with very poor luck enticing members of the opposite sex to be interested in him. It frustrated him, and he began to think

A woman visits a memorial near the Albertville secondary school in Winnenden, Germany, after Tim Kretschmer went on a rampage at his old school.

that women were laughing at him behind his back. This paranoia manifested itself in his interest in sadomasochistic pornographic scenes that featured women humiliating men. According to police reports, he actually watched one such video within minutes of leaving his home to go commit murder.

Despite the depression, video game obsession, and awkward teenage blues, there seemed to be no inkling that Kretschmer was so close to the psychotic break that would turn him into a notorious murderer.

On March 10, 2009, he stole a gun from his father's locked collection, left a rambling suicide note on the Internet, and went back to his old school, where he proceeded to kill fifteen people including nine students—the majority of which were girls. Unlike most mass murderers however, Kretschmer tried to get away. In fact, he carjacked a Volkswagen and ordered the driver to go for several hours, hoping to pass another school. When the driver spotted a police car, he opened his door and jumped from the vehicle.

Kretschmer engaged the police in a short shootout before killing himself.

Warning signs:

Loaner, gaming addiction

Pattern of attack:

Used gun to shoot victims

Number of victims:

Sixteen, including himself

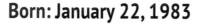

Born: January 22, 1983

Occupation: Student

Diagnosis: Unknown

Died: April 26, 2002, suicide

Robert Steinhauser, another German school shooter, is perhaps the most unique of the bunch. While he may have exhibited signs of anger and maybe even some depression, for the most part he appeared normal before his killing spree. He is also unique in that he clearly targeted teachers, not fellow students. It appears he was driven by a carefully hidden internal darkness and revenge.

Steinhauser was born to middle-class parents in a working-class neighborhood in Germany. Things changed when his parents divorced when he was about twelve years old. Friends and psychologists speculated that listening to his parents disagree and openly argue for years before splitting may have affected him more than he let on.

Steinhauser started spending more time alone. He also became very interested in learning about World War II and all things military. If he idolized Hitler—as some other school shooters have—it went virtually unknown. There were no posters of the fascist leader in his room, but there were posters of supermodels. The one social interest he had was shooting. He belonged to a gun club and the only friends he really had were other members. He owned his own gun.

A police tape marks the area outside the Gutenberg High School in Erfurt, Germany, on the day after former student Robert Steinhauser, armed with two weapons, entered the school and killed sixteen people.

He did have anger issues—or at least issues with authority. He was argumentative, hated to be corrected, often talked back to teachers, and was known to be disrespectful at times. His anger issues got worse when he failed a standardized test at his high school that was necessary to pass in order to attend a university or get a decent job. Upset at his lack of prospects, he skipped school for a few days and then submitted a forged medical note when he returned. The school expelled him.

Steinhauser was devastated and could not tell either of his parents. He got up every morning and pretended to go to school. No one knows what he was doing during the time he was supposed to be in school.

On April 26, 2002, Steinhauser returned to his school with murder on his mind. He brought his gun as well as a change of clothing—all black—with a ninja mask. He changed his clothes in one of the school's bathrooms and then the carnage began.

He went from classroom to classroom, targeting teachers and administrators. He killed two students inadvertently when he fired his gun through locked doors. He also shot and killed a police officer from the window of the school.

The carnage ended when a teacher confronted Steinhauser and told him to shoot him, but only if he took off his mask. When Steinhauser removed it, he told the teacher there would be no more killing. It was as if the mask allowed him to be someone different, someone murderous. The teacher then pushed Steinhauser into a room where the nineteen-year-old shot and killed himself.

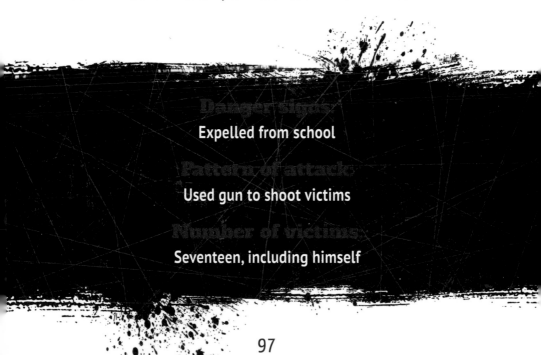

Danger signs:

Expelled from school

Pattern of attack:

Used gun to shoot victims

Number of victims:

Seventeen, including himself

Chapter 5

More
SHOOTINGS

This final chapter takes a look at random school or public shootings. Those profiled were chosen based on their diversity. There is a killer who suffered from Asperger's syndrome, another who was motivated by hatred and bigotry, and a narcissist who committed the deadliest public shooting to date.

We've seen some patterns emerge: loneliness, poor social skills, broken homes, and at times, fascination with other mass murderers, Hitler, or some other type of fascism. Still, we are left wondering why. In truth, there are many different types of motive for mass murder, ranging from revenge to despair to free-floating rage at the world. Some people develop visions of annihilation, while others seek headlines. For the Aurora incident, we should allow time for a proper analysis. The shooter himself may not realize the many threads that wove into his stunning act of violence.[1]

For the most part, public places and schools are filled with innocent people. In a way, targeting children in school is the ultimate disgrace—a total and complete slap at society. In their twisted way of thinking, the killers may choose these targets for that same shock and outrage factor. "Now maybe something might be done, some sort of change or reform," they might be thinking. Even terrorists know this. Ever wonder why the Palestinian terrorists shoot missiles at Israel from schools or hospitals? It's simple. They want Israel to retaliate by knocking down a school and injuring innocent children. They know it will outrage the world. The children in this case—like in the cases of school shooters—cease being human but simply pawns, a means to an end. In the end, we are equipped with more information than ever before—more warning signs, symptoms, and coping mechanisms. But what we are still left with is that terrible one-word question: Why?

Not every schizophrenic kills. Not everyone with Asperger's goes on a shooting spree. Not every person suffering from antisocial disorder and depression idolizes Hitler.

Many times we look for a solitary reason or cause and this is a mistake. When someone plans violence of this magnitude, the motives generally simmer for a long time until they reach a boiling point. Perspective that could help us understand and prevent these crimes takes time and patience.[2]

What can be learned from the following killers?

Born: July 26, 1989
Occupation: Student
Diagnosis: Asperger's syndrome
Died: October 1, 2015, suicide

Christopher Harper Mercer was obsessed with guns for as long as anyone who knew him could remember. As a child growing up in southern California, he would often wear the same green army pants and combat boots for days in a row. He barely spoke, unless the topic had something to do with guns or the military. It got worse the older he became. In the weeks, days, and hours before he went on a shooting rampage at a community college in Oregon, he was spending more and more time on online message boards. He would describe his loneliness, his inability to get a girlfriend, and just grew more and more despondent.

Mercer was born in Great Britain to Owen Mercer and Lauren Harper, a mixed-race couple. They moved to the United States when he was relatively young and they split up when he was sixteen. Mercer lived with his mother, a nurse practitioner who suffered from Asperger's syndrome just like her son. She worked hard to shield him from loud noises and things that irritated him. One time, she went through her entire building asking her neighbors to sign a petition to force the building owner to spray for cockroaches. She went around telling everyone that her son had mental issues and the roaches were irritating him very much.[3] She would also knock on neighbors' doors if their televisions were too loud or if their dogs were barking too much. Loud sounds annoyed him.

One loud sound that did not bother Mercer was gunfire. His mother had a passion for guns and shared her hobby with her son. His face would light up when someone brought up the topic.

Mercer attended community college and graduated with a degree in a special program designed for students with autism. After graduation he tried joining the army, but he flunked out of basic training and came back home.

Mercer stated often that he was opposed to organized religion and expressed affinity for the Irish Republican Army. Like many of the other killers we've read about, Mercer's late teens and

Chris Harper Mercer went on a shooting rampage at Umpqua Community College. He killed ten people and wounded seven more.

early twenties were filled with a sudden fascination with school shootings, public shootings, the idea that killing can make you famous, and Nazis. He supposedly ordered components of a Nazi officer's uniform on the Internet and used German military terms for his screen name on a dating website.

That's the other thing Mercer had in common with many of the other killers: he was a virgin, something that bothered him greatly. He moved to Oregon with his mother two years before the attack. He had told people he was looking forward to a fresh start. It never happened.

On the morning of October 1, 2015, Mercer went to Umpqua Community College, where he was enrolled, and started shooting. He was armed with six guns, body armor, and lots of spare ammunition. He killed nine people before police began firing at him. He shot and killed himself.

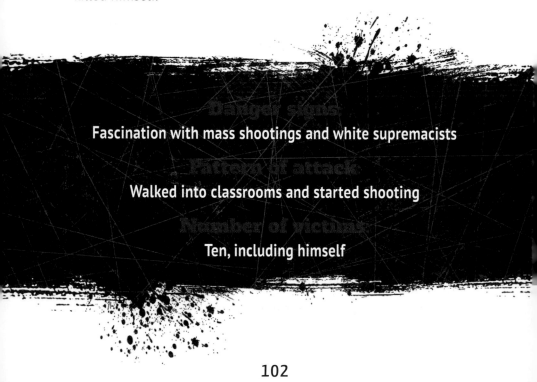

Danger signs

Fascination with mass shootings and white supremacists

Pattern of attack

Walked into classrooms and started shooting

Number of victims

Ten, including himself

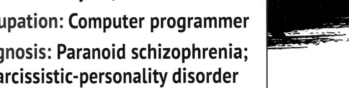

Born: February 13, 1979

Occupation: Computer programmer

Diagnosis: Paranoid schizophrenia; narcissistic-personality disorder

Using car bombs and then automatic firearms, Anders Breivik claimed twenty-seven lives in Norway. If asked, he would probably tell you that he's good at everything. No, he would tell you that he's better than you. That's because Breivik is one of the most extreme cases of narcissistic-personality disorder that psychologists have studied. But they warn that society, in general, is becoming more narcissistic. And that can be dangerous.

Psychologists say that narcissism is on the rise. Feeling left out and excluded is normally at the center of the narcissist's pain. Their response to the shame of losing or of being excluded is sometimes violence, which serves two purposes: It enacts revenge while also taking the perpetrator out of oblivion and making them "somebody."[4]

Breivik's childhood was not even close to being conducive to a normal upbringing. His mother and maternal grandmother were both paranoid schizophrenics. His father, a Norwegian diplomat, was said to be cold, harsh, and cruel.

The moment Breivik was born, his mother sank into a depression that never seemed to go away. In fact, raising Breivik and his half-sister was simply too much for the sick mother. She hired a young

Anders Breivik, a self-confessed mass murderer, appears in court for killing seventy-seven people.

couple to watch the children on weekends. The mother encouraged her son to explore his sexuality with his weekend father. It's no wonder that he was sent to see a child psychologist at a young age.

According to reports, Anders was described in case notes as "aggressive and nasty." He had no friends and exhibited a lot of antisocial behaviors, such as destroying flowers and throwing rocks through windows. He would also torture his pet rats, and when he grew taller he took great pleasure in bullying younger children.

He joined a gang and started vandalizing property by spray painting graffiti. When he outgrew the gang, he turned his attention to a political party with staunch right-wing views regarding immigrants, taxes, and socialism. When his rise up the party's ladder was stymied, Breivik secluded himself in his mother's house where he became obsessed with violent video games and anti-Muslim websites filled with conspiracy theories.

The self-styled fascist began a computer programming business in order to fund a long-term project of murder and mayhem. He told police that he started planning and saving up for the deadly 2011 attacks back in 2002. He bought guns, ammunition, and the ingredients for a bomb.

On July 22, 2011, his murderous plan was set in place. He blew up a government center killing eight people and diverting many emergency responders. Then, dressed as a policeman, he took a ferry to Utoya Island where there was a youth camp for the country's Labour Party—the party that he blamed for the country's problems. He began firing on the children methodically, one after another. He even found some children pretending to be dead and he shot them through the head. He killed sixty people on the island before his arrest.

Norwegian police continue their search for victims on Utoya Island after Anders Breivik went on a shooting spree.

Psychoanalyst Otto Kernberg described the extreme case as malignant narcissism. He called it the source of much "evil in the world." When reality is disappointing, the love turns inward and the person starts to idolize themselves. They excuse bad behavior and tend to do a lot of admiring. This type of narcissism becomes deadly when destructive impulses take on a noble or moral feel in their conscience.[5]

Danger signs

Became withdrawn and isolated

Pattern of attack

Car bomb and then mass shooting

Number of victims

Seventy-seven

> **Born: October 11, 1942**
>
> **Occupation: Unemployed security guard**
>
> **Diagnosis: Sought help for unknown mental health issue**
>
> **Died: Killed by police on July 18, 1984**

James Huberty may be the most tragic mass murderer profiled in this book. He knew there was something wrong with him and actually sought help. When it didn't come, he snapped and went on a murderous rampage.

Like many of the killers, Huberty had a difficult childhood. He contracted polio at the age of three, and even though he was able to recover, he had difficulty walking the rest of his life. When he was about ten years old, his father decided to buy a farm in Pennsylvania's Amish country. His mother was unhappy there, though, and abandoned the family to become a street preacher.

Huberty seemed normal enough growing up but had problems sometimes making decisions. He went to college for sociology but switched to mortuary school before eventually becoming a welder. He met his wife in college, and the couple had two baby girls in the early 1970s.

His personality changes were subtle. He became violent with his wife at times, though some described him as a good family man. He also started thinking that the family should isolate themselves,

Gunman James Huberty suspected something was wrong with him. Unfortunately, he snapped before he got help. He killed more than twenty people at a McDonald's restaurant.

as he became involved in the survivalist movement. He became very paranoid about the Russians and Soviet aggression. He began accumulating guns and became more and more fascinated with war.

In 1982, his world came crashing down when he lost the welding job he had held for more than ten years. He was worried that the bank would take his house away and leave his family homeless. He moved his wife and two daughters to Mexico, and they loved it. He did not love it, though, and moved the family to San Diego, California. In San Diego, Huberty became despondent. His wife once walked in on him as he held a small handgun to his head. She pried the gun from his hands and went to hide it. He remained on the couch weeping.

Neighbors described him as unhappy and irritable, someone who was quick to argue. To Huberty's credit, he was able to recognize that there was something wrong with him. He told his wife he was calling a mental health clinic in order to make an appointment to get some help. She later told police that he sat next to the phone all day long waiting for a call back. But none came, and that may have been the final straw on this fragile man's mind. He felt worthless, so low that he didn't even deserve a call back.

The following day, he drove his car to a McDonald's restaurant after telling his wife he was going hunting for humans. He entered with an Uzi and a shotgun and began targeting Mexican Americans, blaming them for him losing his job a year earlier. A police sniper finally ended the carnage when he shot and killed Huberty.

Danger signs

Told wife he had mental problem and sought help

Pattern of attack

Drove to restaurant and started shooting

Number of victims

Twenty-one

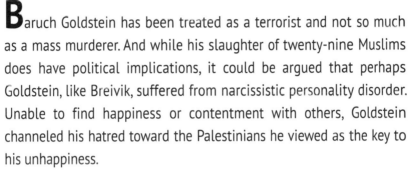

Born: December 9, 1956

Occupation: Physician

Died: Beaten to death on February 25, 1994

Baruch Goldstein has been treated as a terrorist and not so much as a mass murderer. And while his slaughter of twenty-nine Muslims does have political implications, it could be argued that perhaps Goldstein, like Breivik, suffered from narcissistic personality disorder. Unable to find happiness or contentment with others, Goldstein channeled his hatred toward the Palestinians he viewed as the key to his unhappiness.

Goldstein was born to an orthodox Jewish family in Brooklyn, New York. He attended Jewish religious study classes, Hebrew School, and then finally medical school at Albert Einstein College of Medicine. He started practicing medicine, specializing in emergency and trauma care, found a wife, and started a family. But those who knew him well were aware that somewhere down the line, Goldstein had become radicalized. He was in fervent opposition to peace deals struck between Israel and the Palestinians and was constantly berating the Arab world. He joined the Jewish Defense League and other organizations, some of them with radical ties.

Eventually he took his family with him to live in Israel where he continued practicing medicine at a local trauma center. He lived

Dr. Baruch Goldstein opened fire on worshipers in the Cave of the Patriarch Mosque on February 25, 1994. Twenty-nine people were killed and more than fifty wounded in the attack, which sparked widespread riots. Baruch was beaten to death by survivors on the same day.

in a part of the West Bank that was known for being a hotbed for anti-Arab sentiment.

In New York, Goldstein had become a follower of a rabbi named Meir Kahane, who was known to preach violence against Arabs, and later led a local chapter of Kahane's followers. When Kahane was assassinated in New York in 1990, Kahane swore revenge against the Arab militants who killed him. While his feelings and beliefs were resolute, it is not clear if Goldstein would have ever carried out such a violent act had a certain incident never occurred.

In December of 1994, three months before Goldstein's murderous attack, his pager went off, indicating a hospital emergency. As the head of the trauma center, Goldstein was needed immediately to help with some badly injured victims of an ambush by Arab extremists. When he arrived at the hospital, he was devastated to learn he would be trying to save the life of his best friend, Mordechai Lapid, and Lapid's nineteen-year-old son. He tried desperately to save them, but they were too badly injured. His friend's son took his last breath in Goldstein's arms.

He was never the same after that tragedy and coworkers would later describe his behavior as sometimes "batty." Perhaps he was batty and perhaps he had suffered a mental break, but Goldstein planned his February 25, 1994, attack at the Cave of Patriarchs very carefully. It was a Friday during the Muslim holy period of Ramadan. He knew the Cave of Patriarchs would be filled with hundreds of Muslim Arabs offering prayers.

Disguised as an Israeli soldier, Goldstein forced his way in and began firing. He was able to get off one hundred shots before being stopped. One of the intended victims knocked him down by bashing his head with a fire extinguisher. Once he was down, Goldstein was beaten to death by others.

He killed twenty-nine people and injured nearly sixty others, though some insist that Israeli security forces may have fired into the crowd, initially thinking the attack on Goldstein to be unprovoked. Extremist groups praised Goldstein for the killings, which were condemned by most of the civilized world.

Danger signs:

Hatred toward Palestinians

Pattern of attack:

Went to a cave and shot Muslim pilgrims

Number of victims:

Twenty-nine

CONCLUSION

Nazis, virgins, video game fanatics, loners, the bullied, the outcasts, and those who want to be known for doing something incredibly big are among the school shooters and public mass murderers. We've also seen the full spectrum of mental illness and psychological diagnoses attached to these now infamous perpetrators. We've seen Asperger's syndrome, paranoia, schizophrenia, antisocial disorder, narcissism, and others.

We know they are typically men. We know they are typically not popular and spend much of their time alone. We also know that at some point these would-be killers developed a complete lack of empathy. They stopped viewing their intended victims as classmates, friends, peers, or little children. Instead, they saw them as obstacles or a means to accomplish their twisted goals.

There is likely no person capable of empathy who would willingly open fire on a classroom of six- and seven-year-old children.

We also know that there are warning signs. "In most cases, there's a long trail leading up to the actual act of violence," said psychologist Peter Langman.

Yet, despite a list of red flags, psychologists say, it is maddeningly difficult to separate the next school shooter from the millions of other disaffected students who may never go on to kill.[1] Most people with mental illness are nonviolent. Most people who experience something bad at school do not go back and kill their classmates. Something happens along the way, and unfortunately, the warning signs are often ignored. How many profiles did we read in which the killers were loners obsessed with guns, Hitler, and school shootings? That is probably not a good sign, and friends or parents should intervene.

But the other sad reality is that every school shooting that takes place gets ingrained in the minds of someone else and may possibly spawn yet another attack. Because of this, psychologists stress the importance of preventing these massacres before they happen. One step in that direction might be to help the kids who do feel the burden of social isolation and feelings of insignificance, regardless of whether they will ever snap.

"It's not so much to catch shooters, because we know that's very difficult, but actually to address very widespread problems that reach millions of kids," notes Katherine Newman, a sociologist at Johns Hopkins University.[2]

Chapter Notes

Introduction

1. Mark Roth, "Expert s Track the Patterns of Mass Murders," *Pittsburgh Post-Gazette,* April 13, 2009, http://www.post-gazette.com/local/city/2009/04/13/Experts-track-the-patterns-of-mass-murders/stories/200904130098 (accessed March 2, 2016).
2. Larry J. Siegel, *Criminology,* 10th ed. Thomson Wadsorth Publications, University of Massachussetts, 2009. p. 121.
3. Frank J. Robertz, "Deadly Dreams: What motivates School Shootings?" *Scientific American,* August 1, 2007, http://www.scientificamerican.com/article/deadly-dreams/ (Accessed January 2, 2016).
4. Ibid.
5. Ibid.

Chapter 1: Older Cases of School Shootings

1. Theophanes, "The History of Nearly 250 Years of School Shootings in America," Hubpages.com, May 7, 2013, http://hubpages.com/politics/The-History-of-Nearly-250-Years-of-School-Shootings-in-America (Accessed December 29, 2015).
2. Ibid.
3. Judith Yates, "First US School Massacre Was in 1764," Examiner.com, July 31, 2013, http://www.examiner.com/article/first-us-school-massacre-was-1764 (Accessed January 2, 2016).
4. Monty J. Ellsworth, "The Bath School Disaster," 1927, http://daggy.name/tbsd/tbsd-t.htm#ChapterThree (Accessed January 2, 2016).
5. Rebecca Coffey, "Lessons from America's First School Massacre," *Psychology Today,* December 21, 2012, https://www.psychologytoday.com/blog/the-bejeezus-out-me/201212/lessons-americas-first-school-massacre (Accessed January 2, 2016).
6. Ibid.
7. Rene Schlott, "Century of Massacres: Remembering Bremen," *Spiegel Online,* June 20, 2013, http://www.spiegel.de/international/zeitgeist/a-century-after-the-first-school-shooting-in-bremen-a-906996.html (Accessed January 10, 2016).

8. Ibid.
9. David Eagleman, "The Brain on Trial," *Atlantic Magazine,* July/August 2011, http://www.theatlantic.com/magazine/archive/2011/07/the-brain-on-trial/308520/ (Accessed January 10, 2016).
10. Ibid.
11. Greg Weston and Jack Aubrey, "The Making of a Massacre: The Marc Lépine Story," *Ottawa Citizen*, February 7, 1990.
12. Marian Scott, "Coroner's Report on Massacre," *Vancouver Sun*, May 15, 1990.
13. *Thomas Watt Hamilton Biography*, http://www.biography.com/people/thomas-watt-hamilton-232311 (Accessed January 10, 2016).
14. Nick Cohen, "The Life and Death of Thomas Watt Hamilton," *The Independent Newspaper*, March 16, 1996. http://www.independent.co.uk/news/uk/home-news/the-life-and-death-of-thomas-watt-hamilton-1672323.html (Accessed January 10, 2016).

Chapter 2: Columbine

1. Peter Langman, "Columbine, Bullying and the Mind of Eric Harris," *Psychology Today*, May 20, 2009, https://www.psychologytoday.com/blog/keeping-kids-safe/200905/columbine-bullying-and-the-mind-eric-harris (Accessed January 10, 2016).
2. Greg Toppo, "Ten Years Later, the Real Story Behind Columbine." *USA Today*, April 4, 2009. http://usatoday30.usatoday.com/news/nation/2009-04-13-columbine-myths_N.htm (Accessed January 10. 2016).
3. Ibid.
4. Langman.
5. Stephanie Chen, "Debunking the Myths of Columbine, 10 Years Later." *CNN*, April 20, 2009, http://www.cnn.com/2009/CRIME/04/20/columbine.myths/ (Accessed January 10, 2016).
6. Ibid.

7. Bill Briggs and Jason Blevins, "A Boy with Many Sides," *Denver Post Online*, 1999, http://extras.denverpost.com/news/shot0502b.htm (Accessed January 13, 2016).

8. Ibid.

9. Greg Sancier, "Looking into the Minds of Eric Harris and Dylan Klebold," PoliceOne.com, April 18, 2014, https://www.policeone.com/active-shooter/articles/7094927-Looking-into-the-minds-of-Eric-Harris-and-Dylan-Klebold/ (Accessed January 13, 2016).

10. Peter Langman, "Sex, Love and School Shooters: Eric Harris," *Psychology Today*, July 23, 2010 https://www.psychologytoday.com/blog/keeping-kids-safe/201007/sex-love-and-school-shooters-eric-harris (Accessed January 13, 2016).

11. Kevin Simpson, Patricia Callahan, and Peggy Lowe, "Life and Death of a Follower," *Denver Post (*online*)*, May 2, 1999, http://extras.denverpost.com/news/shot0502c.htm (Accessed January 15, 2016).

12. Ibid.

13. Stephen Greenspan, "Murder Most Foolish," *Psychology Today*, February 7, 2011. https://www.psychologytoday.com/blog/incompetence/201102/murder-most-foolish (Accessed January 15, 2016).

14. Ibid.

Chapter 3: Going Postal

1. George Simon, "Going Postal: the Common Denominator." *Counselling Resource*, May 19, 2014, http://counsellingresource.com/features/2014/05/19/going-postal-common-denominator/ (Accessed January 20, 2016).

2. Ibid.

3. Scott Lilienfeld, Steven Jat Lynn, John Ruscio, and Barry L. Beyerstein, "50 Great Myths of Popular Psychology," *Association for Psychological Science*, 2010, http://www.psychologicalscience.org/media/myths/myth_30.cfm (Accessed January 14, 2016).

4. William Robbins, "The Loner: From Shy Football Player to 'Crazy Pat,'" *The New York Times*, August 22, 1986, http://www.nytimes

.com/1986/08/22/us/the-loner-from-shy-football-player-to-crazy-pat. html (Accessed January 16, 2016).

5. Richard Goldstein, "Howard Unruh, 88, Dies," *New York Times*, October 19, 2009, http://www.nytimes.com/2009/10/20/nyregion/20unruh.html?_ r=1 (Accessed January 16, 2016).

6. Ibid.

7. Ibid.

8. Juan Ignacio Blanco, Murderpedia.org, http://murderpedia.org/ male.H/h/hennard-george-jo.htm (Accessed January 16, 2016).

9. Richard Walsh, "The Luby's Cafeteria Massacre of 1991," *Crime Magazine*, April 30, 2015, http://www.crimemagazine.com/lubys-cafeteria- massacre-1991 (Accessed January 16, 2016).

10. Ann O'Neill, Ana Cabrera, and Sara Weisfeldt, "A Look Inside the Broken Mind of James Holmes," CNN.com, June 10, 2015, http://www.cnn. com/2015/06/05/us/james-holmes-theater-shooting-trial/ (Accessed January 16, 2016).

11. Scott A. Bonn, "James Holmes and the Bloody Dark Knight Massacre," *Psychology Today*, March 3, 2014, https://www.psychologytoday.com/ blog/wicked-deeds/201403/james-holmes-and-the-bloody-dark-knight- massacre (Accessed January 16, 2016).

12. Chris Weller, "Two Key Factors Explain Why People Like Dylann Roof Commit Violent Hate Crimes," *Business Insider*, June 22, 2015, http:// www.businessinsider.com/dylann-roof-committed-a-mass-shooting- because-of-trauma-and-exclusion-2015-6 (Accessed January 16, 2016).

13. Katie Zavadaski, "Dylann Roof's Manifesto Is Chilling," *The Daily Beast*, June 20, 2015, http://www.thedailybeast.com/articles/2015/06/20/ dylann-roof-s-racist-manifesto-is-ignorant-and-chilling.html (Accessed January 16, 2016).

Chapter 4: **Post-Columbine**

1. Elizabeth Simers Bowers, "Inside the Mind of School Shooters," *Lehigh University College of Education*, http://coe.lehigh.edu/content/inside- mind-school-shooters (Accessed January 20, 2016).

2. Ibid.

3. Vicki Smith, "Cho's Problems Date to Early Childhood," *USA Today*. August 30, 2007, http://usatoday30.usatoday.com/news/nation/2007-08-30-3532663914_x.htm (Accessed January 20, 2016).

4. David Shortell, "Report Finds Missed Chances to Help Newtown Shooter Adam Lanza," CNN.com, September 23, 2014, http://www.cnn.com/2014/11/21/justice/newtown-shooter-adam-lanza-report/ (Accessed January 20. 2016).

5. Ellis, Ralph, "Adam Lanza's Father in First Interview: He Would Have Killed Me in a Heartbeat," CNN.com, March 10, 2014, http://www.cnn.com/2014/03/10/us/adam-lanzas-father-speaks/index.html (Accessed January 20, 2016).

6. Peter Langman, "Revisiting Adam Lanza: The Official Sandy Hook Report," *Psychology Today*, November 29, 2013, https://www.psychologytoday.com/blog/keeping-kids-safe/201311/revisiting-adam-lanza-the-official-sandy-hook-report (Accessed January 20, 2016).

7. Associated Press, "Minnesota School Shooter Called Self 'Angel of Death,'" *USA Today*, March 22, 2005. http://usatoday30.usatoday.com/news/nation/2005-03-22-shooting-suspect_x.htm (Accessed January 20, 2016).

8. Juan Ignacio Blanco, Murderopedia.org http://murderpedia.org/male.K/k/kretschmer-tim.htm (Accessed January 20, 2016).

Chapter 5: **More Shootings**

1. Katherine Ramsland, "Mass Murder Motives," *Psychology Today*, July 20, 2012, https://www.psychologytoday.com/blog/shadow-boxing/201207/mass-murder-motives (Accessed January 20, 2016).

2. Ibid.

3. Jack Healy and Ian Lovett, "Oregon Killer Described as a Man of Few Words, Except on Topic of Guns," *New York Times*, October 2, 2015. http://www.nytimes.com/2015/10/03/us/chris-harper-mercer-umpqua-community-college-shooting.html?_r=0 (Accessed January 22, 2016).

4. Anne Manne, "Narcissism and Terrorism: How The Personality Disorder Leads to Deadly Violence," *The Guardian*, June 8, 2015. http://www.theguardian.com/world/2015/jun/08/narcissism-terrorism-violence-monis-breivik-lubitz-jihadi-john (Accessed January 22, 2016).

5. Ibid.

Conclusion

1. Tia Ghose, "The Psychology of Mass Shootings," *Livescience*, December 19, 2012, http://www.livescience.com/25666-mass-shooting-psychology.html (Accessed January 22, 2016).

2. Ibid.

Glossary

abomination—Something horrible that causes disgust.

allegation—An accusation that someone has done something wrong.

annihilation—Complete destruction.

carnage—The massacre or killing of a lot of people.

commence—To begin or start something.

condemnation—Punishing or criticizing someone very harshly.

exclusion—Omitting something or someone.

indiscriminately—Done with no rhyme or reason.

malignant—Something spiteful or malicious.

manifesto—An in-depth mission statement.

mechanism—A natural, accepted process that normally results in an expected outcome.

methodically—Done in a precise, planned order.

narcissism—Excessive love of oneself.

neuroscience—The science of studying the brain and nervous system.

oppressive—Designed to keep someone down or enslaved.

supremacist—Someone who believes one race is far better than any others.

vandalize—To damage property on purpose.

Further Reading

Books

Castledon, Rodney. *Spree Killers: The Enigma of Mass Murder.* Canary Press, 2011.

Hickey, Eric. *Serial Killers and Their Victims.* Belmont, CA: Wadsworth Publishing, 2012.

Langman, Peter. *Why Kids Kill.* New York: St. Martin's Press, 2009.

Latta, Sara. *Medical Serial Killers.* New York: Enslow Publishing, 2016.

Newman, Katherine S. *Rampage: The Social Roots of School Shooting.* New York: Perseus Books, 2004.

Rauf, Don. *Female Serial Killers.* New York: Enslow Publishing, 2016.

Woog, Adam. *Careers in the FBI.* New York: Cavendish Square, 2014.

Websites

The Federal Bureau of Investigation
fbi.gov/stats-services/publications

Reports and publications regarding the study of violent criminals including serial, spree, and rampage killers.

Psychology Today
**psychologytoday.com/blog/wicked-deeds/201407
/why-spree-killers-are-not-serial-killers**

Read about the difference between spree killers and serial killers.

School Shooters.info
schoolshooters.info

Resources on school shootings, perpetrators, and prevention.

Index